ENDORSEMENTS

Steve and I have been personal friends of Mark and Lizzie over many years. We have humbly watched them embrace this journey of conceiving, loving and, ultimately, having to release their beautiful baby Keziah back to God.

Keziah – A Little Piece of God's Heart is etched with grief and joy, loss and enrichment, inner strength and hope. It will inspire you to discover more of the character and presence of God that is unswerving and unchanging in the midst of painful storms.

Mark and Lizzie's tenacious determination to cling to Hope and the perspective of heaven has spoken powerfully into my heart. I believe their story has the capacity to touch and influence the lives of countless others.

Lizby Warren
Senior Pastor and College Principal, C3 Church Amsterdam

Keziah is the heart-rending story as told by mother Lizzie during her forty-one-week pregnancy which ended tragically in her beautiful baby girl Keziah being stillborn. Lizzie has gracefully managed to capture this journey throughout the highs and the lows, the tears and the laughter, the sorrows and the joys. This is not just a book but a healing and comforting "Guidebook to Hope" to help anyone who has suffered the same tragic loss of a child. Each page has been thought over and poured into with wisdom for life springing from the unchanging Word of God, which Lizzie and her husband Mark have fastened themselves onto. They have shown incredible strength, dignity and courage in the face of adversity. Their faith and absolute trust in God amidst the pain of grief and disappointment should challenge and inspire us all. Thank you for sharing your story in order to give others a "Hope" for the future. Keziah has left her own legacy even after only nine short months here on earth. To God be the glory.

Lara Martin, Songwriter, Worship Leader

A truly inspiring, encouraging and compelling read for anyone who has experienced the emotions and feelings which accompany the undesirable episodes of disappointment, bereavement and grief in their life.

If you have ever wondered how anyone could ever move on after the loss of a child, this book gives a well-written account of how faith, hope and love are essential tools in the process of healing and restoration after such an event.

For Christians it highlights the importance of drawing on the strength of God's love and promises in times of trial and tribulation whilst providing an opportunity for non Christians to discover the peace that emanates from having faith.

As an Obstetrician, I have the privilege of caring for women during pregnancy, often a time filled with joy and the excitement of looking forward to the birth of a new life as indeed most pregnancies are normal. However, when medically untreatable conditions (such as lethal chromosomal conditions) complicate a pregnancy, it not only brings such unimaginable distress to the woman affected and her family but also causes frustration for the medical personnel as they can feel helpless.

Keziah not only helps families touched by this in showing how to cope with the various emotions that might be encountered but also highlights the critical role health professionals must play in supporting these families in their decisions.

I highly recommend this book to any woman and her family who have been affected by pregnancies with chromosomal abnormalities or any other severe complications that appear untreatable. I shall also recommend it as an invaluable reading material to my colleagues in the speciality.

Mr Adeyemi Ogunremi MBBS, MFFP, FRCOG
Obstetrician & Gynecologist

I initially met Lizzie and Mark after they had been seen in the antenatal clinic by one of my colleagues at the Princess Royal University Hospital as I was, at the time, managing the clinic. This amazing couple were coping with an extremely bewildering time as their unborn child had been diagnosed with Edwards syndrome.

I was immediately struck by their serenity and an aura of calm that surrounded them as we sat and talked in a busy clinic. This was the start of my journey with Keziah which has been so beautifully portrayed in this book *Keziah: A little piece of God's heart*.

Throughout my contact with Lizzie and Mark I was and still remain humbled by their faith and unconditional love for their baby. Their serenity as they went through a journey knowing that they would be returning their daughter to God's care so soon was remarkable and again humbling to those of us who have had the privilege of having children and watched our dreams for them unfold.

Having been a midwife for thirty years I am eternally grateful for all that Lizzie and Mark have taught me as I watched and wept with them as they embraced Keziah's journey.

Alison Eagle, Midwifery Manager, PRU site SLHT

Having known the author for a number of years we can vouch for the authenticity of this account. Her story is real and a "must read" for those experiencing a rough time in any area of their lives.

Pastors Alan and Lydia Vance
Senior Pastors, bcc – The church

As Lizzie's "earthly" father I want to commend this book to you. Life is not always easy and Lizzie's journey with Keziah was such a time. During her pregnancy her total confidence in the assurance of Philippians 4:13, "I can do everything through Christ, who gives me strength," was, and is, a wonderful testimony to how her "heavenly" Father provided for her during this difficult time. As I prayed with Liz, while we were holding Keziah in our arms, that God would show us His purpose in taking her from us, she told me that this was not for us to know but for God alone. We know that God causes everything to work together for the good of those who love Him and are called according to His purpose (Romans 8:28), and that Keziah's birth and death will be used to His glory. Great is His faithfulness! His mercies are new every morning! We rejoice in our new granddaughter Iona as testimony to this!!

Roy Kemp
International Treasurer, UK Chairman SAT–7 Trust

Well before her launching into this detailed and intimate account of her encounter with God, during His taking from her, at the time of birth, her long-awaited daughter – I had known Lizzie for many years.

My wife (Lillie) and I often prayed for and sometimes with her. In the most natural way, she had a unique "flavor" for and with children and young people. Even today, her overflow in relationship with young people is a work of the Holy Spirit. Whether abroad or in the East End of London, in her calling the power of the Holy Spirit has been constantly at work in and through her.

This biography of hers is indescribably moving, incredibly uplifting, uniquely encouraging and undeniably exemplary!! On prayerfully reading this, you will discern her not only living in the Spirit, but expressing the life of the Spirit while under every kind of spiritual pressure. This is a true story and account that will help bring you to more fully have the character of the Lord – the very purpose of your knowing the Savior!

If even the Apostle Paul personally yearned to know the Lord and to experience the fellowship of His sufferings, it is so timely and fitting in these end days for us all to have this opportunity of treading that "upward pathway" (Philippians 3:14)!

Ken Burnett , Founder, Prayer for Israel

The loss of a loved one is always painful, but the loss of a child is even more devastating. Mark and Lizzie Grayson had the added trauma of discovering early in the pregnancy that their much-anticipated unborn baby had severe abnormalities and, in the opinion of the medical experts, could not survive.

This book tells with moving candour the journey they made to the birth of their stillborn infant. It is a story of faith triumphing in the darkest of times, and it testifies that God's promises to His children never fail.

Peter Mawson, Co-pastor, Headley Park Church, Bristol

Keziah

Keziah

A little piece of God's heart

Lizzie Grayson

Sovereign World

Sovereign World Ltd
PO Box 784
Ellel
Lancaster LA1 9DA
England

www.sovereignworld.com

Unless otherwise stated, Scripture quotations are taken from the New International Version (NIV). Copyright © 1973, 1978, 1984 by International Bible Society. Published by Hodder & Stoughton Ltd.

The following versions are also used: New Living Translation (NLT). Copyright © 1996, 2004 by Tyndale Charitable Trust. Used by permission of Tyndale House Publishers. Amplified Bible (AMP). Copyright © 1954, 1958, 1962, 1964, 1965, 1987 by The Lockman Foundation.
Kind James Version (KJV).

Grateful thanks to the following songwriters and publishers for permission to use their lyrics: Nicole C. Mullen for "Redeemer," © 2000 Lil' Jas' Music (adm. P&P Songs Limited, 40 St Peter's Road, London W6 9BD): Wordspring Music/Word Music Group (adm. by Song Solutions CopyCare, 14 Horsted Square, Uckfield, East Sussex, TN22 1QG.info@ songsolutions.org); Brooke Ligertwood (née Fraser) for "This is My Prayer Desert Song," copyright © 2008 Brooke Fraser/Hillsong Publishing/kingswaysongs.com; Kate Simmons and Mark Edwards for "Creation Song," copyright 2000 Little Room Music/Administered by 1Q Music; Beci Wakerley and David Wakerley for "As the Sun Comes Up My Number One," copyright © 2007 David Wakerley & Beci Wakerley/Hillsong Publishing/kingswaysongs.com; Brooke Ligertwood for "I will exalt you," copyright © 2009 Ligertwood/ Hillsong Publishing/kingswaysongs.com.
And to Destiny Image for permission to use extracts from *The Supernatural Power of a Transformed Mind - 40-Day Devotional and Personal Journal* by Bill Johnson and *Christianity in the Crosshairs* by Bill Wilson, copyright © 2006 and 2004 (respectively), used by permission of *Destiny Image Publishers*, 167 Walnut Bottom Road, Shippensburg, PA 17257 www.destinyimage.com.

ISBN 978 1 85240 540 3

The publishers aim to produce books which will help to extend and build up the Kingdom of God. We do not necessarily agree with every view expressed by the authors, or with every interpretation of Scripture expressed. We expect readers to make their own judgment in the light of their understanding of God's Word and in an attitude of Christian love and fellowship.

Cover design by Simon Watkins, www.vietnamthemovie.co.uk
Typeset by Hurix
Printed in the United Kingdom

Dedicated to anyone who has ever had a stillborn.

In memory of Keziah Esther Joy Grayson
24 September 2008

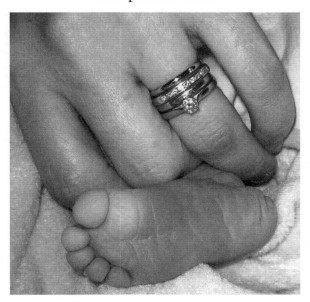

CONTENTS

FOREWORD BY BILL WILSON

As someone who understands what tragedy in one's life means, Mark and Lizzie's story really hits close to home. It's easy to blame God and walk away when tragedy strikes. That's what most people do. But they chose to depend on God in the midst of everything. This book will challenge you to take a deeper look into the core of your being. It will encourage you to have a greater dependency on Him and His Word in the most difficult moments of your life.

Mark and Lizzie's story is unforgettable. They have truly understood what Jesus meant when He said in Matthew 11:28-9,

> "Come to me, all you who are weary and burdened, and I will give you rest. Take my yoke upon you and learn from me, for I am gentle and humble in heart, and you will find rest for your souls."

Bill Wilson
Senior Pastor and Founder Metro Ministries

ACKNOWLEDGMENTS

First and foremost, I want to thank God for not only giving me life and salvation, but also for helping me complete this book.

I want to give special thanks to my husband Mark for his love and for standing with me throughout and giving me three beautiful children: Josh, Keziah and Iona.

I want to add a special thankyou to my parents and also to each member of our family on both sides, close and extended, plus the many amazing friends that God has brought into my life. Many of you are mentioned by name because of a special part you had to play in my life throughout my time with Keziah. I do hope I haven't offended anyone in any way if your name is not in print! If you are part of my world, then know that I love you!

Finally, I would like to thank everybody who prayed for us from the moment we knew there was a problem with the pregnancy. I believe the strength and grace we received were a direct result of the prayers of many believers who carried us in their hearts.

Thank you.

INTRODUCTION

There is a way through

Every birth is a miracle. Each pregnancy is unique, a life-changing journey for those intimately involved. For some the journey is easy and smooth. For others it may be littered with obstacles and unwanted roadblocks. Many find that the journey is over just as soon as they realized they'd taken the first step. I have traveled a few of these journeys.

My first pregnancy ended for us at the twelve-week ultrasound, when we were informed that the pregnancy sac was empty (blighted ovum). My second pregnancy culminated in the joyful arrival of our son Joshua. Two years later, a few days after Joshua's second birthday, on 24 September 2008 at 1.57 pm I gave birth to our daughter Keziah Esther Joy Grayson. She was stillborn. Six months later, I returned from hospital, this time after an ERPC (Evacuation of Retained Products of Conception). We had found out two days previously that this next baby (my fourth pregnancy) whose heartbeat was strong at eight weeks, viewed at a dating scan, had soon after died in my womb. By God's grace, we found the courage to pick ourselves up and try again. My fifth pregnancy brought healing and restoration as we welcomed another daughter, Iona, into the world.

Five journeys, five pregnancies, only three that arrived at the final destination. For one of these, the scenery on arrival was not as expected. This is the story of that journey, Keziah's journey. At times my journey with Keziah was heart-breaking, but the one defining factor that enabled me to walk with strength and dignity was the presence of God.

"Let the beloved of the Lord rest secure in him,
for he shields him all day long,
and the one the Lord loves rests between his shoulders."
                                                    (Deuteronomy 33:12)

There is a wonderful security that comes when you know that you are loved. A secure place, a shelter, a refuge, a haven. A place to run to, a place to hide, when the circumstances of life seem overwhelming. To run into the arms of my Heavenly Father, whose love was as real as any friend's yet even more so, was my daily refuge. To sit quietly and be overwhelmed by His love: there I found shelter, my haven, the place I ran to.

The pain of losing a child is sometimes so suffocating that you wonder how you will survive the next breath, let alone the rest of your life. But there is a way through. A path can be taken which, although dark, confusing and unknown, can be showered with sheer joy, all-consuming peace and transforming hope. It's a path that demands a choice because if left to chance, it will be easily missed. The first few steps are the hardest but when the rewards outweigh the pain of discipline, each step becomes easier.

I wanted to write this book to give hope to anyone who finds themselves traveling along a journey similar to ours, because even though you may be totally unaware of them right now, I promise you there are always "treasures of darkness, riches stored in secret places" (Isaiah 45:3) to be found. The purpose of these treasures is discovered in the next part of that verse: "so that you may know that I am the Lord, the God of Israel, who summons you by name."

My prayer is that you may come to a place where heaven's perspective is your landscape. That, through fresh eyes of faith, you can see the privilege of being given a little piece of the Father's heart, as He chose and entrusted you, for however long or short, to look after your child that returned to His arms.

> May the God of hope fill you with all joy and peace as you trust in him, so that you may overflow with hope by the power of the Holy Spirit.
>
> (Romans 15:13)

You will find as you read through *Keziah* that verses from the Bible play a prominent role in our journey. This is because I truly believe that the Bible is the Word of God and a powerful way in which God still speaks today. I unashamedly leant on each truth to gain daily strength and courage. You may not share my faith, yet I would like to personally thank you for taking time out to read part of my life story. I would encourage you to read with an open heart and mind, wherever you may currently stand on issues of faith. There is a beautiful cry of God's heart recorded in the book of Hosea, chapter 6 verse 6: "I want you to know me" (NLT). May that be your experience as you read through *Keziah*.

Lizzie

Chapter 1

YOU ARE NOT ALONE

———————————~~~~/———————————

Because he has set his love upon Me, therefore will I deliver him; I will set him on high, because he knows and understands My name [has a personal knowledge of My mercy, love, and kindness – trusts and relies on Me, knowing I will never forsake him, no, never].

(Psalm 91:14 AMP)

The 1st of May 2008 is a day etched into my memory. My husband Mark went off to school to teach as normal, while I set off for King's College Hospital, London to have a twenty-week ultrasound scan. My mum accompanied me, with the task of keeping our twenty-month-old son Joshua occupied so that I could enjoy watching our unborn baby in peace. I was totally unaware of what the day would hold. In hindsight, I now understood the concerns that were raised two months earlier at the twelve-week scan when I was told there was a 1:56 adjusted risk of Trisomy 13 / 18. In my ignorance I didn't realize the significance of this. The sonographer was foreign, speaking English very quickly with a heavy accent, and just kept mentioning extra chromosomes. She had reassured me that the baby didn't have Down's syndrome and, as that was the only chromosomal disorder I was aware of, I'm ashamed to say that I had taken completely no notice of her ramblings and had left the twelve-week scan blissfully unaware of any problem and totally happy in my ignorance.

Back to 1 May. Like any excited mum-to-be, I watched with pride as the sonographer started to look at the baby, pointing out some of the vital parts! I was enjoying the peace and quiet of the room and making the most of the opportunity to lie down alone in the middle of the day without being clambered over by a lively toddler.

In my enjoyment of the peaceful ambiance, I didn't notice at first that the sonographer had gone very quiet and was repeatedly meticulously studying the baby. Half an hour passed and, after wearing down a path in the outside corridor chasing Josh up and down, my mum poked her head around the door to check that all was OK. I hadn't been told otherwise so assured Mum that I was fine and would be out soon. The original sonographer had disappeared to get reinforcements and shortly returned with another professional to aid her with her inspection. By this time, I was beginning to suspect that all was not well. My suspicions were sadly confirmed.

The second specialist gently explained that they had found several abnormalities with the baby. He/she had a large hole in the heart, narrow arteries, cysts on the brain, a bone missing from the upper arm and extra digits on the hand. All of these symptoms were conducive to one of two conditions: Trisomy 13 or 18 which, we were told, medically speaking are known as lethal chromosome conditions.

Our experience throughout the whole pregnancy was that the medical profession gave us no hope whatsoever that our unborn baby would live and the words "lethal chromosome condition" were reinforced at every possible opportunity. The professional opinion was that the baby probably wouldn't survive the pregnancy and if I did carry full term, he/she either wouldn't survive labor or wouldn't live long if born. There was no life expectancy at all.*

While this was all being discussed, I was taken into another room to be given a second ultrasound scan by a cardiologist. She explained that if the heart problems were in isolation, they could operate when the baby was born. However, if they were symptoms of Trisomy 13 or 18, the choice to operate would not be given, as the life expectancy was zero. It was all too much to take in. A minute ago I had been excited, looking at our baby moving about in the womb, and now I was being told he/she had severe abnormalities and would not survive.

In retrospect, I think it is quite shocking that having just been hit with horrendous, unexpected news and in a very emotional state, you are given the option to terminate the pregnancy there and then, as if it is a minor problem that can just be dealt with by a simple operation. Considering the possible long-term psychological and emotional effects of choosing to terminate a pregnancy, nothing about it is simple. To terminate the pregnancy was not an option for me. I was adamant. My decision on this particular matter had been made long ago.

I had loved this baby since before conception, seen him/her alive and kicking at twelve weeks, carried him/her in my womb for twenty weeks and enjoyed the wonder of nurturing a new life growing inside me. I didn't consider that it was my choice to end this baby's life, whatever I was being told.

I was encouraged to have an amniocentesis so that the doctors could identify specifically whether the baby was

---

* Later information supplied to us by SOFT UK Support Organisation for Trisomy 13 / 18 and related disorders made us aware of many children that had lived into adulthood and SOFT both dislike and disagree with the term "lethal chromosome condition."

suffering from Trisomy 13 or Trisomy 18. They explained that amniocentesis is one of several diagnostic tests that can be carried out during pregnancy. It is used to detect any possible chromosome abnormalities in the unborn child that may cause Down's syndrome or other congenital problems. In amniocentesis a sample of the amniotic fluid that surrounds the fetus is removed and analyzed. This test is performed from week 15 of the pregnancy onwards. By this stage I had phoned Mark to explain to him what was happening and he was on his way up to be with us.

After agreeing to the amniocentesis, I was led to a quiet room to wait for Mark and sit and process the news by myself. Ironically, out of all the rooms set apart for this purpose, I was led to the same room we had been put in almost three years previously in August 2005 when, at the twelve-week scan, we were told that our first pregnancy hadn't taken and the pregnancy sac was empty.

Mark had been with me then, this time I was alone. Well, not quite! In the stillness of the room, while I sobbed in anguish over what we had just been told, I made myself stop. I suddenly thought that this was no surprise or shock to the God who holds my life in the palm of His hands.

I remembered reading the story of how Darlene Zschech, the worship leader from Hillsong Church, Australia, after having a miscarriage sat in her car, letting the tears flow as she began to worship her Heavenly Father. I had also heard Lara Martin, an accomplished songwriter and worship leader, speak at our church of her many miscarriages. Despite their devastating circumstances, both women made the choice to look up, to worship and to walk with their God through the storm.

It was so hot in the little room and I was emotionally shattered, yet I knew God was with me. I sat there with tears streaming down my face and made myself sing over and over again the words of a simple Lara Martin song, "You never fail me! You never fail me, Lord."

If any of the doctors had walked past, they would have thought I was totally crazy, sitting there alone, singing as loudly as I could! Nevertheless, I knew that God was with me and only by running to Him could I find the strength I needed to face each moment of our unknown path ahead.

Years previously, while working as a missionary throughout my twenties, the transition had been made from my head down to my heart that God loved me. A simple but totally life-transforming truth had awakened something at the core of my being. Identity, purpose, security and strength followed the knowledge that through the cross of Jesus I had been given the privilege of becoming a daughter of the Most High God!

"The Lord your God is with you, he is mighty to save.
He will take great delight in you,
he will quiet you with his love,
he will rejoice over you with singing."

(Zephaniah 3:17)

This was one of my all-time favorite truths from the Bible as the revelation of its meaning had changed my whole perspective on the character of God and how He felt about me personally. I simply believed what it said and the results of that simple choice were life changing.

Over the years I had enjoyed more and more the pleasure of seeking God and experiencing His tangible love. On our wedding day, 24 July 2004, Mark and I vowed that we would "seek God's presence as the foundation of our home." I thanked God that the foundations had been laid previously and at that moment, sitting alone in the room when it seemed that our lives were crumbling around us with the news we had just received, I knew that we would be OK. Whatever the outcome, we were not alone.

Mark came straight up to the hospital and sat with me during the amniocentesis. My dad had also traveled up to help us with Josh and eventually, along with Mum, we all left the hospital. Josh was blissfully unaware of any change in our circumstances, but we four adults were too shattered emotionally to say much and were all trying in our own way to process the news.

That night, Mark and I lay in bed, held hands and sang the old hymn "Our God Reigns." We had just read a passage from our evening devotional book, the verse from Psalm 91:14 quoted at the start of this chapter. We knew that whatever we were to face in the coming months, we would get through it and be stronger for it. God had promised not to leave us or forsake us. We both had that personal knowledge of God's mercy, love and kindness. We chose together to trust and rely on Him at this crisis point in our lives. Our prayer from that day was that God would use our lives, our journey, for His glory and that others would come to know of His love and faithfulness. We were not alone.

Chapter 2

LOOKING UP...

But you are a shield around me, O Lord;
you bestow glory on me and lift up my head.
To the Lord I cry aloud,
and he answers me from his holy hill.

(Psalm 3:3)

The night of 1 May, I could not sleep. My thoughts and emotions were on overdrive. I sat up until 4 am looking up on the Internet each symptom we had been told and finding out as much as I could about Trisomy 13 and 18. None of it was good news. I felt such a heaviness over me as I read other people's stories and cried as I identified with their pain. I knew that I needed to keep the balance between knowing the facts of what we were facing and holding onto the power of the unseen where my strength would come. I eventually got an hour's sleep before Josh woke up at the crack of dawn to start his day. Having to keep going for the little man helped, as there was no room to sit and wallow.

That first weekend when we knew something was wrong but weren't yet totally sure which syndrome it was, was a strange time. We had told close friends and family what had happened at the hospital and already the house resembled a florist's: flowers, cards and texts with messages of support had come flooding in. The Senior Leaders at our church in Bromley, Pastors Alan and Lydia, came around to visit us on the Saturday afternoon. Pastor Alan prayed as they laid hands on me that God would perform a "creative miracle" in the life of our unborn child.

I don't know how, but on the Sunday at church Mark led worship from the platform with a big smile on his face as usual. In contrast, pleased to be hidden by the darkness, I stood and cried all the way through the music. The lack of sleep, hormones and emotions were all taking their toll!

It was Bank Holiday weekend and the weather was gorgeous. We'd planned a family day out up in London on the Monday, just the three of us. It was a special day just to be together and enjoy each other's company without having to explain our circumstances or even face the sympathy of others. We had decided that not everybody needed to know what was happening. I was at the time running four weekly sessions of "Shake, Rattle and Rollover," a 45-minute music class for mums and babies I had created, developed and set up, plus two half-days of flute teaching. I wasn't looking forward to standing and facing a roomful of people on Tuesday morning but knew it had to be done. I needed to carry on with some semblance of normality for as long as the pregnancy allowed.

I was very aware of my fragility, yet at the same time so thankful that I didn't have to walk in or rely on my own strength. One of my heroes from Israel's history who has inspired me for a long time, is King David. I love the fact that he was described as a "man after God's heart" (1 Samuel 13:14). I'd always had a lot of fun teaching children from the Bible about David's adventures with his God. For the eleven years prior to Josh's birth I had worked for London City Mission and then for our church, "bcc – The church." My main role was as a Children's Pastor, going into local schools and taking assemblies and clubs, teaching the Bible through fun methods. King David's actions thousands of years previously were now to be my guide to help me face the coming months.

When faced with an extremely difficult situation in his own life, the Bible describes his secret weapon in nine short words in 1 Samuel 30:6: "But David found strength in the Lord his God." At that particular time in his life, he strengthened himself. No one else did it for him. He did it himself. His secret became my daily action! I knew that if I kept choosing to acknowledge that God's presence was far bigger than any problem we faced, I would be OK.

My first key, then, was to make sure that I sought out God and stayed in His presence. My favorite way to do that was to sing and sing loudly! Psalm 22:3 explains that God "inhabits the praises of his people" (KJV) – inhabits, dwells, lives, comes to stay. If someone comes to stay at your house, their presence is obviously felt by you. To praise Him, then, means to experience His presence and in His presence there are many benefits. Psalm 16:11 became my constant mantra:

You have made known to me the path of life;
you will fill me with joy in your presence,
with eternal pleasures at your right hand.

During that first weekend, I gathered together a small selection of my favorite God songs. Each song focused on the character of God, capturing His greatness and power, yet expressing His tenderness and ability to empathize with me and our situation.

I didn't want to live under the heaviness of despair, and that decision drove me to a place where I knew joy was waiting and available. Isaiah 61:3 sets a "spirit of despair" against "a garment of praise." A garment is something you put on.

A coat will not jump off the hanger from your wardrobe and appear on your back. Just as it takes a physical act to get dressed in the morning, I knew that as I chose to put on daily my "garment of praise," I could shake off the despair and replace it with joy. The first thing I did every morning was to switch on the Ipod and let the music wash over me, soothing my tender emotions to bring peace to my spirit.

The words of one particular Nicole C. Mullen song, "My Redeemer Lives," encouraged me every day. They spoke of daily victory through the one who had conquered death and is alive. With Him, I could face each tomorrow.

Who taught the sun where to stand in the morning?
and Who told the ocean you can only come this far?
and Who showed the moon where to hide 'til evening?
Whose words alone can catch a falling star?

Well I know my Redeemer lives
I know my Redeemer lives:
Let all creations testify
Let this life within me cry
I know my Redeemer lives, yeah.

The very same God that spins things in orbit
runs to the weary, the worn and the weak
And the same gentle hands that hold me when I'm broken
They conquered death to bring me victory...

Because He lives I can face tomorrow
I know I know
He lives He lives yeah, yeah I spoke with him this morning.

That first week, I didn't feel like singing, but I knew that in the Kingdom of God the right feelings follow the right action. Passivity never changes anything.

My second key was to meditate on God's promises and speak them out loud over my life and our circumstances.

I knew the power of confession. In Proverbs 18:21 the Bible teaches:

> The tongue has the power of life and death,
> and those who love it will eat its fruit.

Psalm 138:2 explains that God has exalted above all things His name and His Word. Isaiah 55:10-11 teaches us that the Word of God is like a seed which produces good results when released on the earth:

> "As the rain and the snow come down from heaven
> and do not return to it without watering the earth
> and making it bud and flourish,
> so that it yields seed for the sower and bread for the eater,
> so is my word that goes out from my mouth:
> It will not return to me empty,
> but will accomplish what I desire
> and achieve the purpose for which I sent it."

I wanted to keep my thinking and speech in line with God's Word and reinforce life with my tongue! I used my song and my words to create faith in my spirit to shape my daily outlook into a positive one. I collected together some of my favorite promises in the Bible, specific verses which had helped me in the past. For years I have had little notebooks or pieces of card where I have written down specific verses that had touched me and carried them around with me to learn. For the next six months I was to be so encouraged by daily text messages from different friends, sending me verses to help and strengthen me. Each one was like a light in the darkness, an anchor of truth to hold onto, helping me to shape my response to the present situation. The Word of God was a powerful tool that gave me immediate strength. My negative emotions would be subdued as I meditated and spoke out loud something more powerful than they were.

It was really interesting that the previous Sunday at church, we had been encouraged to write down a list of times when God had broken through into our lives. I did this straight away (during the preach!), so totally missed the rest of the message. With a growing sense of excitement, I wrote down the first ten instances that came immediately into my mind. These were occasions when God had spoken directly into my world. There were many more but this was a good starting point.

Being able to look back over my life and remember challenging times, yet knowing that God had brought me through gave me great confidence. God had never failed me and He hadn't changed! I knew that if I kept looking up, lifting my eyes, hands, head and heart to the one who had promised to see me through to victory, instead of looking at the problems, real as they were, I could face each day with strength.

In the book of Jude Paul encourages his readers to "build yourselves up in your most holy faith and pray in the Holy Spirit" (v. 20). Years previously, whilst studying music at York University, I had contracted a viral infection that led to a diagnosis and personal battle against ME (chronic fatigue syndrome). During my battle with this illness I had been challenged after reading a book called *Chasing the Dragon* by an extraordinary woman called Jackie Pullinger (Hodder & Stoughton, repr. 2010). Jackie saw God do many miracles amongst drug addicts in Hong Kong and supernatural happenings were a daily occurrence. I decided to follow her example and discipline myself to sit and pray in tongues (the language of the Holy Spirit) for fifteen minutes a day.

It was a discipline that always drew me closer to God and gave me an increased awareness of the Holy Spirit and His power living within me. I'm ashamed to say that I had grown lazy in using this gift. Now was the time to revive it. This was another key to use in my current battle.

The final thing that I knew to do was simply to obey the short commands in 1 Thessalonians 5:16–18:

Be joyful always; pray continually, give thanks in all circumstances, for this is God's will for you in Christ Jesus.

If our joy is dependent on the circumstances, then it will waver and fluctuate according to external change. If we choose to focus on the one who is unchanging, then we are able to obey that command. There is such power in the last part of this command. Again, I remembered teaching a kids' club on "the attitude of gratitude" based on this verse. I had so much to be thankful for. Firstly, my salvation and the knowledge of God with me, then so much else!

I remember just after the first failed pregnancy in August 2005, the year before Josh was born, I sat and wrote down 100 things I was thankful for in my life. Well, that list has grown since then. Being thankful for an amazing family and fantastic friends plus the very fact that I was pregnant and the baby was still alive at twenty weeks, helped me to focus on the positive.

Chapter 3

Trisomy 18

Consider it pure joy, my brothers, whenever you face trials of many kinds because you know that the testing of your faith develops perseverance. Perseverance must finish its work so that you may be mature and complete, not lacking anything.

(James 1:2-4)

We had been told to expect a phone call with the results of the amniocentesis within five working days. That first weekend we felt a little in no-man's land. Even though they had scanned the baby so thoroughly, there was still a hope in our hearts that maybe the test would be negative and all would be well.

There is something about pregnancy that, even under normal circumstances, seems to turn me into a creature of the night! Throughout the nine months with Josh, nocturnal awakenings were a regular occurrence: during the early hours I had consumed copious amounts of chocolate and viewed countless episodes of *ER*. I was in fact quite amazed that he hadn't come out humming the theme tune!

The day after the Bank Holiday, 6 May, I had woken up some time after midnight with James 1:2-4 (quoted above) going round in my head. I know that when we sleep, our bodies may be resting but our spirit is awake. Psalm 16:7 explains it in this way:

I will praise the Lord who counsels me;
even at night my heart instructs me.

The nocturnal whisperings of the Holy Spirit are so precious to me. There is such a special intimacy shared when everyone else is asleep, the house is completely quiet, the atmosphere is still, and it's just you and God. It makes the lack of sleep worth it! Both Mark and I were aware that this trial was the biggest test of our faith so far. Although I may not have liked the nature of the trial, I certainly liked the promised result: "maturity and completion/wholeness, not lacking anything." Little nuggets of gold like this were like solid anchors, immovable truths to latch on to when circumstances were shaky.

The phone call came that evening. It was earlier than we had anticipated and so, although expected, the timing took us by surprise. Mark was just on his way to speak at our young adults' meeting at church. He answered the phone, then handed it to me, saying it was "The Harris Birthright Unit" from King's Hospital. The phone call was short and to the point. On confirming my identity as Mrs Grayson, I was told that the results of the amniocentesis had tested positive for Trisomy 18. The lady asked me if I understood what that meant. I replied that I had done some research, so was aware. She explained that 50 per cent of Trisomy 18 babies didn't survive pregnancy and the other 50 per cent didn't survive birth. She then told me that I could expect to go into labor at any time from that point. It was a very impersonal phone call. She simply explained the facts, informed us we had an appointment the next day at the Princess Royal Hospital when we could discuss any questions, and put the phone down.

I sat staring at the phone and burst into tears. The glimmer of hope we'd had earlier that maybe the diagnosis would be different than the scan had suggested, disappeared. It was too late for Mark to find someone to cover him, so he gave me a quick hug and left.

I wasn't amused and just sat there for ages, in slight shock. I phoned my parents, but couldn't speak through my tears, so just packed Josh in the car and drove around to their house. Fortunately, they live five minutes away. We didn't speak much when I arrived, just shared lots of big hugs and tears while we bathed Josh and got him ready for bed.

That night I was wide awake again. Now armed with the definite knowledge of what we were facing, I re-read all I could about Trisomy 18. The Trisomy 18 Foundation website seemed like the most accurate source of information. It confirmed and expanded the brief knowledge I had been given in the phone call. With kind permission, they have allowed me to quote what I read that night:*

"What causes Trisomy 18?"

At conception, 23 chromosomes from the father and 23 chromosomes from the mother combine to create a baby with 46 chromosomes in each cell, two of each type. Each chromosome holds a particular "position" in the cell and carries certain genetic material. A trisomy occurs when a baby has three chromosomes in one position instead of the normal two.

The most common trisomy is Trisomy 21, also known as Down Syndrome, where a baby has three of the twenty-first chromosome. Trisomy 18 is the second most common trisomy and occurs when a baby has three of the eighteenth chromosome. This results in 47 chromosomes instead of the normal 46 in the affected

---

* The extract is taken directly from www.trisomy18.org

cells. It is this extra genetic material that causes the problems associated with Trisomy 18.

Trisomy 18 is also called Edwards syndrome and occurs in about 1:3000 live births. Unlike Down Syndrome, Trisomy 18 is usually fatal, with most of the babies dying before birth and those who do make it to birth typically living only a few days. However, a small number of babies (<10%) live at least one year.

Most trisomies (about 95%) are full trisomies. That is, the extra chromosome occurs in every cell in the baby's body. This type of trisomy is not hereditary and is not due to anything the parents did or did not do.

"What are the characteristics of Trisomy 18?"

The extra genetic material from the additional eighteenth chromosome can cause a variety of problems with varying severity. Just as children with Down Syndrome can range from mildly to severely affected, so can children with Trisomy 18. Therefore there is no hard and fast rule what Trisomy 18 will mean for your child. However, statistics show that there is a high mortality rate for children with Trisomy 18 before or shortly after birth.

Some of the typical characteristics of Trisomy 18 can include heart defects such as VSD (Ventricular Septal Defect – a hole between the lower chambers of the heart), ASD (Atrial Septal Defect – a hole between the upper chambers of the heart), and coarctation of the aorta (a narrowing of the exit vessel from the heart), kidney abnormalities, omphalocele (a portion of the intestinal tract is located outside the stomach in a sac), esophageal atresia (the esophagus does not connect to the stomach, meaning the baby cannot eat by mouth) and polyhydramnios (excess amniotic fluid), clenched hands, choroids plexus cysts (a pocket of fluid on the brain that is not problematic in itself but may be a marker for Trisomy 18), rocker bottom feet, and delayed growth, micrognathia (small jaw), low-set ears, and a strawberry-shaped head, as well as severe developmental delays.

The statement "there is no hard and fast rule what Trisomy 18 will mean for your child" stood out for me. As I looked through the legacy pages on the website, it was apparent that no one story was the same. We didn't know how long the pregnancy would continue, whether our baby would be one of the few who lived to see his or her first birthday or whether we would hold him or her in our arms alive.

That night, before I eventually went to sleep, I read the words from my Dad's favorite Psalm 139. Verses 13-16 in particular gave me great comfort:

> For you created my inmost being;
> you knit me together in my mother's womb.
> I praise you because I am fearfully and wonderfully made;
> your works are wonderful,
> I know that full well.
> My frame was not hidden from you
> when I was made in the secret place.
> When I was woven together in the depths of the earth,
> your eyes saw my unformed body.
> All the days ordained for me were written in your book
> before one of them came to be.

I went to sleep bathed in peace. Amidst the uncertainty, my God was my Rock.

Chapter 4

KEZIAH ESTHER JOY GRAYSON

—————————— ∿ ——————————

*The second daughter [he named] Keziah...Nowhere in
all the land were there found women as beautiful as Job's
daughters...*
(Job 42:14-15)

Mark and I arrived at the Princess Royal Hospital (PRU)
the following afternoon. We were ushered into a room to
see a consultant and sat wondering what he would say. His
opening words came as a surprise. He looked at us both and
said in an apologetic tone, "I'm very sorry to hear that your
daughter has tested positive for Trisomy 18."

Our daughter! Our baby was a girl! Mark and I stared at
each other briefly in surprise and I let out a tiny smile. Our
daughter!

The impact of this news caused me to switch off momen-
tarily to what the consultant was saying. A daughter! I already
knew her name: Keziah. The first time I had heard the name
Keziah was about eight years ago. I had really loved it and
decided if I ever had a daughter, that is what she would be
called. Mark took a little persuading but we had an agreement
when I was pregnant with Josh: if it was a boy, Mark got to
choose the name; if it was a girl, then the decision was mine.

Joshua Daniel Isaac Grayson was born on Friday 15 September 2006 at 2.23 am. Now, for however long she was with us, we had Keziah. For a split second, and this sounds awful to admit, I did wonder if we should save the name in case we had a healthy girl in the future, but that idea just didn't seem right and I dismissed it as quickly as it came. For literally years I had carried the name Keziah in my heart, praying that one day I would have a daughter. Now she was alive in my womb. Later that afternoon, when I told my mum the baby was a girl, she burst into tears, thinking it made it harder for me. Strangely, I felt the opposite. I actually found it a great comfort that I was carrying our daughter.

I knew that unless we had a miracle she was not expected to live, yet that afternoon, sitting in the hospital, I was twenty-one weeks' pregnant and she was alive inside my body.

In Ephesians 1:4 the Bible speaks about God choosing us "in Christ before the creation of the world." There's a beautiful line in the Creation Song written by Kate Simmonds that says,

Long before the world began I saw your faces,
    I knew your names
Just like a father loves his child, that's how I love you,
    so much love for you.

(From the album *One Day*)

Just as we were conceived in love in the heart of God before we ever existed, I felt I had already loved Keziah even before she was conceived. Now she was here: her heart was beating; she was a tiny living being.

I do believe there is great significance in choosing names. We chose Josh's first two names after Joshua and Daniel in the Bible. We loved what these men of God stood for and achieved. Isaac simply means "laughter" and it suits Josh perfectly. Keziah's names were chosen with similar care and thought.

Keziah means "cinnamon" or "warm spice." It was the name of Job's second daughter, born in the latter part of his life when God restored to him all he had lost as a result of Satan's testing of him. I loved the fact that his three daughters were described as women of great beauty. Keziah's second name was to be Esther. Esther is one of my favorite women in the Bible. She was brave, beautiful, not afraid to take risks, and rose up to fulfill her destiny and take her place in history. She was a beauty queen whose courage and bravery saved the Jewish nation, her people, who were about to be annihilated by an evil man called Haman. Esther's cousin Mordecai supported, guided and counseled her to be strong in the face of great danger, saying:

> "And who knows but that you have come to the kingdom for such a time as this and for this very occasion?"
>
> (Esther 4:14 AMP)

A whole book in the Bible is named after her and tells her story.

I chose Keziah's last name to be Joy. Joy is my middle name and, as a tomboy growing up, I hated it as it seemed far too feminine. I changed my mind as I grew my hair and grew up! Nehemiah 8:10 says, "Do not grieve, for the joy of the Lord is your strength." I haven't always walked in it, but the older I am, the sheer joy of knowing Jesus has been and is so precious to me. It seemed apt to name her this as I knew that each time I chose to seek God and trust in His love, His joy would follow. Keziah, inside me, would sense it too and enjoy her time inside! I remember doing a hilarious assembly, years previously, in a junior school in East London with my friend Ruth. We both had cushions stuffed up our jumpers as we acted out the event in the Bible when Mary, the mother of Jesus, met her relative Elizabeth who was pregnant with John the Baptist. Luke 1:41-44 states,

When Elizabeth heard Mary's greeting, the baby leaped in her womb, and Elizabeth was filled with the Holy Spirit. In a loud voice she exclaimed: "Blessed are you among women, and blessed is the child you will bear! But why am I so favored, that the mother of my Lord should come to me? As soon as the sound of your greeting reached my ears, the baby in my womb leaped for joy."

I have always found this amusing, but now it took on greater significance with respect to the life of an unborn child and his or her ability to sense and react to surrounding circumstances. In John 15:9, 11 Jesus says,

"As the Father has loved me, so have I loved you. Now remain in my love…I have told you this so that my joy may be in you and that your joy may be complete."

Jesus expected that His joy in us would be part of our experience of knowing Him. I wanted Keziah to have joy as part of her experience too.

During our appointment that afternoon, we were given a plan of action to follow until I went into labor. We booked to have another scan the following week and from then on we would see Miss Wright,* Head Obstetrician, fortnightly. An appointment had also been set up to see Dr Craig Turner, Pediatrician, who would be involved with aftercare if Keziah survived the birth. There were so many "ifs." When we finished with the consultant, we met Sarah Hartson, Head Midwife. She sat down with us in the corridor and asked if we had any further questions. We were touched by her simple act of kindness in taking the time to sit down and get to know us during this

---

* All names have been changed to protect the identities of the professional medical staff at the PRU Hospital, Locksbottom, Kent.

bewildering time. We asked if she had any experience with Edwards babies,[†] in order to advise us in the journey ahead. She respected our decision to continue with the pregnancy and commented on our serenity. She remarked on the rarity of Edwards babies being born as most people chose termination after diagnosis. She wrote in our file that we had named the baby Keziah. Both Mark and I were impressed with her professionalism combined with such a lovely personal touch. She was one of several incredibly special people we were to walk Keziah's journey with. That afternoon we learnt afresh the value of a smile, a gentle touch and sympathetic ear which can never be underestimated.

[†] See p. 38.

Chapter 5

SING

I will praise you, O Lord, with all my heart;
I will tell of all your wonders.
I will be glad and rejoice in you;
*I will **sing** praise to your name, O Most High.*

(Psalm 9:1-2, emphasis mine)

In between hospital appointments and scan days, life carried on as usual. May has always been my favorite month of the year, as even in England where the weather is so unpredictable, we tend to get at least a handful of beautiful sunny days. During the week when I wasn't working, Josh and I went out and about with friends and family as much as we could. A lovely friend, Judi, from church offered her services as our gardener and during the warm weather, while she worked in the garden, I enjoyed watching Josh potter about, soaking himself with water. His laughter was so infectious and countless times I thanked God for the gift of his life and the joy he gave us as parents.

Mark's life was not so relaxed. Working full time as a secondary school teacher, he would have loved to laze about in the garden and relax. He was having to deal with the daily stresses of his job as well as carrying in his heart the awareness of what was going on with our unborn child.

One evening when we were talking, Mark shared his perspective on what we were facing. He was also drawing wisdom and strength from the life of David who had, like us, faced a life-and-death situation with one of his children. In 2 Samuel 12, the account of David's child with Uriah's wife is given. When the child becomes ill, David pleads, prays and fasts before God for his life. Sadly, the boy dies but, knowing how inconsolable the king had been during the illness, David's servants are too afraid to tell him. On learning that the child has died, however, David confuses his servants by his actions. He gets up, gets dressed, eats and worships in the house of God. In 2 Samuel 12:21-23 we read:

> His servants asked him, "Why are you acting in this way? While the child was alive, you fasted and wept, but now that the child is dead, you get up and eat!"
>
> He answered, "While the child was still alive, I fasted and wept. I thought, 'Who knows? The Lord may be gracious to me and let the child live.' But now that he is dead, why should I fast? Can I bring him back again? I will go to him, but he will not return to me."

David was a worshiper long before he became king and the habit of running into God's presence to give Him praise was a hallmark of his life. His offering of worship got him through good and bad times. David chose to worship and trust God when things happened that he didn't understand and when circumstances failed to turn out according to his desires.

One of Mark's gifts is to lead people into the presence of God through worship. He started playing keyboard and singing in church at the age of thirteen and has been involved in varying roles since then. Unknown to me, during the first month of receiving news about Keziah, Mark had sat down at the piano and composed a song. When he first played it to me, I was amazed!

Throughout the rest of the pregnancy, we were to sing it often together at home and subsequently with our church, bcc – The church, after Mark introduced it one Sunday when he was part of the music team. It's called simply "Sing."

Your ways are higher than mine,
Hope and healing come from Your hands.
Walking side by side,
from the valley to the mountain,
I will worship You.

Thank You, You'll never let me go.
Thank You, Your grace and mercy flows!

I will sing of Your majesty, sing of Your love,
I will sing of Your faithfulness, forevermore.

I will lift my hands and raise my voice,
Proclaiming my God, how great You are!
How great You are!
How great You are!

All the time that Keziah was alive, we would pray and ask God for the miracle of complete healing that we knew He had the power to do. Having experienced several miracles in my body, I had the confidence that this could happen again for Keziah.

As a young child, I had many problems with my ears, nose and throat, which in turn affected my hearing and speech. At the age of seven I was given a hearing aid to wear. I was in and out of hospital for various operations, culminating in a new eardrum being grafted into my left ear when I was eleven years old. This improved my hearing but I relied heavily on lip reading and my hearing aid (when I actually put it on!). When I was eighteen, after being prayed for by a friend, I received the baptism of the Holy Spirit. God touched me unexpectedly, and instantaneously my ears were completely healed. I have never since needed to wear a hearing aid. I contacted the ENT specialist who had seen me since childhood and asked for a hearing test to confirm what had happened. He was utterly amazed that I responded to the test with one hundred per cent accuracy. He had no other explanation than to believe my testimony that God had touched my life and completely healed me of my previous hearing problem!

As a teenager, after undergoing various blood tests and scans I was also diagnosed with polycystic ovary syndrome, a condition which I had been told could seriously affect my ability to conceive children. During the first year of our marriage, I decided to tackle this problem with prayer and fasting as I really wanted to have children and I didn't want this condition to stand in our way. My mother-in-law Helen and I were regularly meeting to pray together, so we began to ask God to again touch and heal my body. After one particular time of prayer and fasting, I knew something had happened and believed God had answered our prayers. This was confirmed by a scan at the local hospital. The next month, I was pregnant with Josh! God heals today: I am living proof!

Around this time, two different people recommended the author Bill Johnson to me. I was eager to devour anything that would strengthen my faith and was really encouraged by the first one of his books that I read. By coincidence, it was also based on the life of David and I was really encouraged as many of the principles written to "strengthen yourself in God" I was already doing. He mentioned others that I also took on board. Although I've never met him, through his teaching Bill Johnson became one of my "spiritual mentors."

As the end of May approached, thankfully so did the half-term holiday and Mark was able to have a short break from his normal routine. It was also his twenty-ninth birthday. We decided to take the bull by the horns and celebrate in style by hosting a big birthday barbecue in the garden. It was a glorious sunny day and a wonderful chance to celebrate life and enjoy the moment. Days like that were special and cherished. Watching Josh play with his friends and spending time with people we love was a wonderful distraction. It was great therapy. Once again, the attitude of thanksgiving helped to chase away the menacingly dark clouds that hovered overhead. These were never far away, threatening to consume every moment with darkness, if allowed to invade the territory of our emotions.

During that half-term week we also went on our first shopping trip for Keziah. With mixed feelings, we picked out a few tiny pink and white outfits. We were determined to believe the best and wanted to prepare for her arrival into the world. As we wandered around the baby department with all the other pregnant women and expectant fathers, I remember consciously avoiding people's eyes as the odd tear escaped silently from mine. I felt the strange tension of faith. We were standing on the truth of God's Word, yet were conscious of the doctors' diagnosis and test results of Trisomy 18. It made me look at other pregnant women differently. I would never assume that just because they appeared happy on the outside, all was well with their baby. Those thoughts had never occurred to me during my pregnancy with Josh.

At times like that, self-pity would try and invade my emotions. It was like an unwelcome visitor, determined to take residence in my soul. I remembered a useful piece of advice a church leader had given me years previously. "If you're going to have a Pom party, you'll have it on your own!" What was "Pom"? Poor Old Me! I took that advice seriously and was careful to stand against self-pity. It was a battle of the mind and will. Without the power of the Holy Spirit living in me, willing me to make the right choices and sustaining the discipline to do so, I know I wouldn't have had the strength to overcome all the negative attacks. In 2 Corinthians 10:3-5 it says:

> For though we live in the world, we do not wage war as the world does. The weapons we fight with are not the weapons of the world. On the contrary, they have divine power to demolish strongholds. We demolish arguments and every pretension that sets itself up against the knowledge of God, and we take captive every thought to make it obedient to Christ.

At the right time, the Holy Spirit would constantly bring scriptures to mind that I had memorized, giving me the weapons I needed to fight. As it says in Hebrews 4:12,

> For the word of God is living and active. Sharper than any double-edged sword, it penetrates even to dividing soul and spirit, joints and marrow; it judges the thoughts and attitudes of the heart.

I used that sword often!

Just as Mark had surprised me with his song, he surprised me again during this holiday week with another practical task he had been working on that I knew nothing about. The previous week, on 20 May, a friend of mine, Karen, had given birth to their first daughter who was born with a congenital heart defect. As Karen and Andy had emigrated to the States, they had set up a fantastic website called Caring Bridge to inform friends and family back home of their daughter's progress. I had shown this to Mark and he had proceeded to set one up for Keziah. I thought it was a brilliant idea as we could keep friends and family posted with any news, along with all the people I knew were praying for us, without having to get in touch with each person individually.

I found it very interesting to see the different ways that Mark and I were handling our current situation. By using our strengths to help each other, I thanked God that already our relationship was deeper and stronger. This was to be one of the many treasures that we dug out of this time.

Chapter 6

BILL WILSON – THE LEGEND!

Even though I walk through the valley of the shadow of death,
I will fear no evil, for you are with me;
your rod and your staff, they comfort me.

(Psalm 23:4)

I have always liked to have something to look forward to and as May ended and June approached, I was getting more and more excited. We are very privileged in our church to be given the opportunity to have our thinking challenged from time to time by external speakers of excellent caliber. Our senior leadership place a high priority on inviting gifted men and women of God to come and share their lives, in order to ignite our hearts and spur us on to a deeper relationship with God. Someone very special was coming to speak on Sunday 1 June and I was so excited!

Since my early twenties I have been involved in numerous different roles at home and abroad in reaching out to children and teaching them about God and His ways. In the spring of 1999, at a Children's Ministry Conference in Eastbourne, I first heard a man speak who totally blew my mind, challenging me more than anyone I had ever heard before. Pastor Bill Wilson, founder of Metro Ministries, New York, is in charge of the largest Sunday school in the world. (Today Metro reaches out to 40,000 children worldwide – a figure that grows daily!) I was completely transfixed as I listened to him speak. Over a decade later, one phrase I heard him say is still with me. He related a visit he had made to an elderly missionary friend who gave him this piece of advice, "If you are ever going to make it, never leave the presence of God." I tucked that away in my mind and have carried it with me ever since. His experiences were profound and his influence on the lives of thousands of vulnerable children immeasurable. All the work I have done amongst children, in schools, weekly outreach clubs and home visits, has been based on the principles he teaches.

In the 1990s the mobile phone company Vodafone ran a series of adverts asking, "Who would you like a 'one-to-one' with?" My answer had been "Pastor Bill Wilson!" In 2005, Mark and I, along with Rob and Caitlin, good friends from church who head up our Sunday children's work, had gone out to visit Metro Ministries and experience the work there first hand. It was incredible. We rode the yellow Sunday school buses, sat in on the sidewalk afternoon sessions in Spanish Harlem, Brooklyn and Queens, went out on visitation and met our sponsor child. We'd met Pastor Bill briefly at the end of their weekly staff meeting, with other guests, but this was different. He was going to be at our church and we would get a chance to sit and chat to him!

The Sunday morning of 1 June, Pastor Bill made us laugh and cry as he related elements of his life ranging from Brooklyn to the garbage dumps of Manila, Philippines. He spoke about Obed-Edom from 1 Chronicles 15, the man who housed the Ark of the Covenant for three months, just so he could be near the presence of God.

Before the evening service, our Pastor, Alan, knowing my love of Pastor Bill, had invited us up into his office to meet him personally. Mark was unfortunately busy at music practice, so it was just Josh and I. Now this rarely happens to me, but when I sat down in front of Pastor Bill, for once in my life I was so awestruck I didn't know what to say! I blurted out, "You're my hero!", not the most subtle start! Pastor Bill was very gracious and didn't make me feel stupid. I didn't stay too long in case I blurted out anything else I would regret!

That night, when Pastor Bill preached, it was just as if God had sent him there specifically for us. He preached on Psalm 23:4, words written by King David (quoted at the beginning of this chapter). Pastor Bill expounded the significance of the rod and staff, explaining that, in Old Testament times, good or bad events would be carved as symbols of remembrance into a person's staff. Defining moments would be marked as personal reminders of what they had been through. The purpose was to be able to look back and say, "God was with me there, He will get me through this now." Both Mark and I were so conscious that my pregnancy with Keziah was a defining moment in our lives.

Through the course of his preaching Bill threw out several nuggets of gold that I captured in my journal, to meditate on later, knowing I would hide them in my heart. As one example, I love this wisdom he shared, "You don't get strength *for* the battle, but strength *from* the battle." Whilst a young shepherd boy looking after his father's flock, David had fought the lion and bear, rescuing the helpless sheep from the ferocious jaws of their enemy. He took that experience and built it into his life, believing that the same God who helped him then would give him the strength he needed to fight Goliath in order to rescue the nation of Israel out of the grip of the Philistines. David had marked his staff: God got me through that, now He will get me through this. It was a direct word from God for us. Mark and I were walking through the valley of the shadow of death with the knowledge of Keziah's

Trisomy 18. God's word and character had never failed us before: His grace would be sufficient for us now.

Pastor Bill was due to speak again to the church the following evening. This time, before the service, Mark was able to come and meet him personally too. After we had chatted, just before we left, I asked Pastor Bill if we could have a photo taken with him. Rob, the friend we'd visited Metro Ministries in New York with, was also there and he had the camera. As he was about to take the photo he asked if we wanted Keziah in it, i.e. my prominent bump! That set me right off.

It just seemed so special that of all the times I should meet Pastor Bill personally, Keziah was there too! I started to cry, Mark started to cry and then so did Pastor Bill! We stood still in a big group hug. I didn't know at that point that Alan and Pastor Bill had had a conversation about what we were going through. I just sensed that he felt our pain and his empathy was straight from his heart of love.

After the meeting, I left clutching one of the 2009 Metro Ministry calendars. I stuck it inside one of our kitchen cupboards and, every morning from that day on, its motto has inspired me to keep persevering with the choice to look up to God: "Your reaction to the struggles of life is a direct indication of your level of vision." If my eyes are fixed on the magnificence of a God to whom nothing is impossible, then my whole perspective cannot help but be brought in agreement with His character. That weekend we had certainly been given additional weapons in our armory to fight whatever came against us on our unknown journey ahead.

Chapter 7

A VERY SPECIAL SCAN

"The bolts of your gates will be iron and bronze,
and your strength will equal your days.
There is no-one like the God of Jeshurun,
who rides on the heavens to help you and on the clouds in his majesty.
The eternal God is your refuge,
and underneath are the everlasting arms.
He will drive out your enemy before you, saying, 'Destroy him!'...
He is your shield and helper and your glorious sword.
Your enemies will cower before you,
and you will trample down their high places."
(Deuteronomy 33:25-27, 29)

With the departure of Pastor Bill, life continued with our normal work timetables. I was coming up to the twenty-fifth week of my pregnancy. We'd had a scan on 14 May and, apart from Keziah growing slightly, there were no changes to report, just a reinforcement of all the abnormalities caused by Trisomy 18. Scan and hospital appointment days were a real battle. I would prepare in the morning by hiding myself in God and asking Him to cover and protect us against the onslaught of medical opinion. These days were very difficult and required extra strength. I refused to give in to fear. One particular scan day, though, actually turned out to be the highlight of the pregnancy.

As it was now a month since we'd first been shocked with the news of Trisomy 18 and I hadn't yet gone into early labor as warned, I started to research an idea that had been forming in my mind. When I was pregnant with Josh, I'd seen an advertisement for 4d scans but decided against having one during that pregnancy. It was quite expensive and we decided to just wait until we met him. This time it was different. Every day that Keziah was still alive within me was a real gift.

I could now feel her moving around inside me and I cherished each movement. I wanted to create as many precious memories of her time with us as possible and the idea of actually watching her in the womb through a 4d scan seemed like a fantastic way to do this. When I told my mum what I was thinking she immediately offered to pay. My parents' generosity is outrageous and they are always blessing us as a family, and my brother's and sister's families as well. I found a private clinic in Hendon, North London that seemed fairly reasonable both in price and in traveling time. I phoned up and explained our situation to the sonographer. She was slightly hesitant at first but patiently listened as I explained why we had chosen to have the scan. Introducing herself as Penny, she graciously said that she had never performed a 4d scan on an Edwards baby before, yet because I sounded so calm as I talked about Keziah, she would agree to do it. I was delighted. By the end of the phone call I felt as if I'd known her for ages! Penny sounded like an absolute sweetheart and I was really looking forward to meeting her. The optimum time for a 4d scan was at twenty-eight weeks, in three weeks' time. We booked our appointment and Penny kindly decided it would probably be a good idea if we were her only clients that afternoon. We would have the entire clinic to ourselves. She wanted us to have the maximum enjoyment possible from the scan and knew we would benefit from a completely relaxed atmosphere. I was so excited and couldn't wait! The date was booked for Wednesday 25 June. I prayed earnestly that Keziah would still be alive and nothing traumatic would happen before that date.

The day before the 4d scan, we had our first appointment with Keziah's pediatrician, Dr Craig Turner. This was interesting. It was an extremely hot day and his tiny office was like a furnace. He was a lovely man and I actually felt sorry for him as he was cast in the role of being the official bringer of bad news. It was his job to prepare us for the worst.

Outlining the effects of a lethal chromosome condition must be one of the more unpleasant aspects of his job. During the whole hour we sat in front of him, he delivered a constant stream of negativity: there was not one piece of good news. It was utterly depressing to hear. His experience of Trisomy 18 babies was exactly what we had read about on the Trisomy 18 Foundation website. In his experience, the condition always resulted in premature death, whether in the womb, during labor or shortly after. I knew Dr Turner was simply doing his job and presenting us with the medical facts, but it made me angry that no alternative view was given. It was completely crazy for me to feel that way – given the danger he must face of being sued by grief-stricken parents – but I felt angry just the same. I sent up a quick "Holy Spirit, help me" prayer and waited. As we sat there and listened, I felt a growing sense of confidence build within me. I remembered the words of Psalm 2 where it talks of God laughing at His enemies because of His supremacy. The phrase "The One enthroned in heaven laughs" (v. 4) was flying round and round in my head. With my ears I was listening to Dr Turner but my mind was elsewhere. I just kept thinking, "Please, God, do it! It will totally blow his mind if we have a complete miracle here!"

I was really pleased that after that appointment we had our 4d scan to look forward to the next day. We woke up to another glorious, hot, sunny day. We dropped Josh off with my parents and caught the train up to London. Mark had the video camera out to capture precious moments and we giggled like teenagers during the journey! My impression after the phone conversation with Penny was confirmed. She was an absolute darling and treated us like royalty. I had taken all my maternity notes with me so that she could read all the doctors' reports and see all the previous scans.

She told us that during the 4d scan she would just concentrate on the positive and skim over anything that might be too upsetting. I lay down on the couch and waited in anticipation. Mark was standing in the corner of the room with the video camera, wanting to capture my reaction as well as filming Penny as she scanned me.

It was absolutely incredible! The first sight of Keziah moving around in the womb was totally overwhelming. She looked completely like Josh! We watched her little facial expressions change, saw her sucking her thumb, smiling and frowning. Her arms and legs were moving around and she seemed to like snuggling up against the corner of the womb. I was crying and laughing simultaneously! It was such an incredible experience. We had chosen the perfect person to scan us. Penny was incredibly sensitive. Unlike previous scans where we'd come away with such a heaviness after being bombarded with all that was wrong with Keziah's little body, she focused on all that was good and made sure we thoroughly enjoyed watching our little daughter. The whole afternoon felt like a very precious gift. On the journey home there was such a lightness in my spirit, a complete contrast to previous hospital visits. I felt as if we had bonded with Keziah. Whatever the future held, that afternoon we had seen our daughter, she was alive and that time spent watching her, we would hold in our hearts probably for the rest of our lives.

Chapter 8

PRAYER TIMES

All glorious is the princess within her chamber;
her gown is interwoven with gold.

(Psalm 45:13)

The same week as the 4d scan, I started following a forty-day devotional and personal journal program by Bill Johnson called *The Supernatural Power of a Transformed Mind* (Destiny Image, 2005). For months Josh had been waking up anytime between 4 and 5.30 am, ready to begin his day with a determination that banished any attempt of mine to remain in the land of nod! I decided to use the time resourcefully! I wanted my thinking to be shaped more than ever by what the Word of God said. I loved the opening quote from day one of the study:

Many of us have treated the will of God as if it's unknown or unknowable...But the will of God is simpler and plainer than we have thought...The will of God is simply this: "On earth as it is in heaven." Isn't that refreshing? When we pray, "Thy Kingdom come, Thy will be done," we're praying for the King's dominion and will to be realized right here, right now...God has not kept His desires secret: He wants the reality of Heaven to invade this rebel-torn world, to transform it, to bring it under His headship. What is free to operate in Heaven – joy, peace, wisdom, health, wholeness, and all the other good promises we read about in the Bible – should be free to operate here on this planet... what is not free to operate there – sickness, disease, spiritual bondage and sin – should not be free to operate here, period.

My constant daily prayer was simply asking God that His Kingdom come and reign in my body.

My primary reason for praying this prayer was, of course, that Keziah would be completely healed of the faulty DNA system that was part of her entire make-up. My secondary reason was the benefits both to me and to those with whom I had daily contact. Romans 14:17 states,

> The kingdom of God is not a matter of eating and drinking, but of righteousness, peace and joy in the Holy Spirit...

I didn't want to live under my circumstances, being a drain to those around me. Instead, I wanted to show the positive difference that knowing God and walking with Him makes to practical everyday life. God is an extravagant Father, who has already made available everything He has to those who choose to know Him and receive what He offers. In Luke 12:32 Jesus teaches,

> "Do not be afraid, little flock, for your Father has been pleased to give you the kingdom."

I was very conscious of the many people who were also praying for both Keziah's life to be touched by God's power and for us to be strengthened throughout this time. I was in constant touch with friends by text who continually encouraged me by sending me different promises that God has given us in His Word. People we had never met but who had heard about Keziah were leaving messages on the Caring Bridge website. We also had a rich spiritual heritage from both sets of parents and their friends. My parents' church, where I had grown up as a child and teenager, were behind us in prayer. Before I'd ever met Mark I had met and become friends with his mum, Helen, at our church. I had also asked her to pray for God to bring along a husband for me, little knowing that her eldest son was to become the answer to that prayer – hilarious! Helen and I often met to pray.

Around the end of June, I decided to bring in the reinforcements and asked Helen and three other close women friends from church – Van, Judi and Rishia – to come over specifically to pray for Keziah to be healed.

We first got together just after the 4d scan and primarily thanked God for Keziah's life and for keeping us strong in Him. We simply presented Keziah before God. These times were a great encouragement to me and provided help for difficult days.

On 9 July (now thirty weeks' pregnant), Josh and I were on our way out to lunch to celebrate Helen's sixtieth birthday when, just before reaching the restaurant, I received a phone call from my dad, telling me that his mum, my Nanny Lou, had just passed away at the age of eighty-nine. Nanny Lou, who was quite a legend, was very loved! Although she had lived a very full life, it was still a shock knowing that she was no longer with us.

The following day, when our little prayer group met up as planned, we had the most beautiful time in the presence of God. After we had spent time seeking Him, we sat in complete silence. The living room was filled with an amazing peace. As I sat there with my eyes closed just enjoying God, it felt as if heaven had invaded our living room and my

womb. The Holy Spirit reminded me of Psalm 45: "All glorious is the princess within her chamber." That seemed a perfect description of our little princess Keziah nestling in my
womb! Nanny Lou was a believer, and I had such a powerful sense of her dancing in heaven (she liked to dance!),
enjoying the presence of God just as we were right then, on
earth. It so comforted me to know that she was perfectly
safe and so indeed was her unborn great-granddaughter.
Our prayer times were special.

In between Nan's death and her funeral the following
week, we had another scan booked at the PRU. It was to be
an interesting appointment! The scan had been requested by
our obstetrician Miss Wright to monitor Keziah's growth.
As we entered the scan room, I saw that the sonographer
already had my maternity notes in front of her.

I handed her the scan request form which clearly stated
Miss Wright's name and the reason for the scan, Trisomy 18.
Having received fantastic treatment from all the medical
profession we had encountered so far, I wasn't prepared
for the reaction of this particular sonographer. I had been
warned by Sarah Hartson (Head Midwife) two months
previously that not everyone would understand our decision to carry on with the pregnancy, but so far we hadn't
encountered any hostility.

We were met with an abrupt question, "What are you here
for?" Considering I was lying there with an enormous belly
whose shape suggested it wasn't the result of over-eating,
plus she had my maternity notes, I thought it was pretty
obvious and was quite surprised. I simply answered what
was written on the form, "Miss Wright requested the scan to
monitor the growth of our baby who has Trisomy 18." She
asked how many weeks pregnant I was, to which I replied,
"Twenty-nine." "How long have you known about Trisomy
18?" was her next question. Not warming to her tone of

voice, I replied, "Nine weeks, we found out at the twenty-week scan." I was wavering at this point between anger and hoping I wouldn't burst into tears. I looked at Mark, who squeezed my hand for silent support. Her next question and the manner in which it was delivered was the last straw, "And you still wanted to continue with the pregnancy?" I stared her straight in the eyes and said, "Obviously! I am now twenty-nine weeks' pregnant and she is our daughter: her name is Keziah." She turned away from me then, and what happened next was so funny it seemed to soften this woman's attitude and completely turn it around.

She stopped in the middle of scanning Keziah and said, "Look, she's smiling at us!" It was incredible! She took a still photo and we have it on our sideboard in a frame. Keziah was looking directly at the camera with her eyes wide open and a big grin on her face!! It was so funny and made me laugh and laugh!

I felt as if we had captured a little piece of her personality on camera and caught a glimpse of her sense of humor. Medically speaking, I'm not sure if any of that is at all accurate or possible, but I'm happy with my interpretation of that afternoon's events and we have the photo to prove it! At the end of the scan, the sonographer actually shook our hands and, smiling, wished us all the best. It was a really odd afternoon.

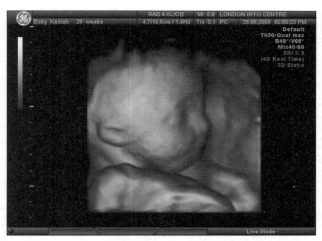

Keziah Esther Joy Grayson, 28 week 4d scan – 25 June 2008 (Chapter 7)

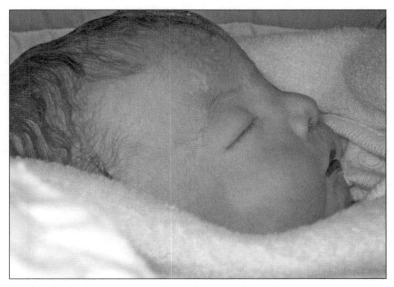

Keziah Esther Joy Grayson – Born 24 September 2008 (Chapter 11)

Mark, Lizzie and Keziah – 25 September 2008 (Chapter 12)

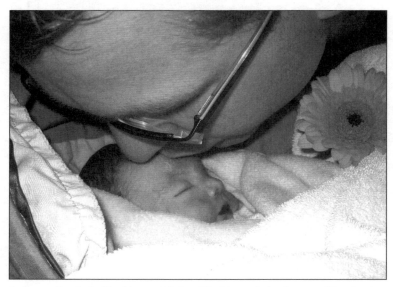

Saying goodbye in the 'Sands' room, Mark and Keziah – 25 September 2008 (Chapter 12)

Scattering Keziah's ashes – Mark, Lizzie and Josh – 31 December 2008 (Chapter 17)

Keziah's 1st Anniversary, Mark, Lizzie and Josh – 24 September 2009 (Chapter 17)

Lizzie and Iona Mia Faith Grayson at 12 weeks, 18 September 2010 (Chapter 17)

Mark, Lizzie and Pastor Bill Wilson, 1 June 2008 (Chapter 6)

Chapter 9

"Do not fear..."

―――――〰―――――

"So do not fear, for I am with you;
do not be dismayed, for I am your God.
I will strengthen you and help you;
I will uphold you with my righteous right hand."
(Isaiah 41:10)

We had now reached the end of term and I had finished my
flute teaching and done the last session of Shake, Rattle and
Rollover. Apart from one scare when I'd ended up on the
floor with a sharp pain in my side, disabling me for about an
hour, I'd managed to carry on (aside from hospital appointments) without cancelling sessions. Many of the mums were
unaware that this pregnancy wasn't proceeding as normal.
I hadn't mentioned what we were facing as I didn't want to
constantly keep speaking out the problem of Trisomy 18,
especially to people who were unaware of the power of
God and His Word. Bill Johnson says that "the way you
see reality is what determines what you think and how you
live...The only way to consistently do kingdom works is to
view reality from God's perspective" (*Supernatural Power of
a Transformed Mind*, p. 21). The Christian life is a journey

in which there is a daily choice to obey the command in Ephesians 4:23-4:

And be constantly renewed in the spirit of your mind [having a fresh mental and spiritual attitude], and put on the new nature (the regenerate self) created in God's image, [Godlike] in true righteousness and holiness. (AMP)

It was up to me to keep my mental attitude fresh. I was hungry to see the supernatural that God promises.

I was officially on maternity leave and my first day happened to be Nanny Lou's funeral. I found the day really emotional. My brother Andrew and eldest niece Sally had come over from Hong Kong and my sister Nicky and her family had traveled up from Devon.

I was supposed to play "Jesus Loves Me," one of Nan's favorite songs, on the flute, but had got so choked up while trying to sing Psalm 23 that I knew I was really going to struggle. I stood up and managed four notes, then burst into tears. I had to sit down and just sobbed my heart out! I felt really stupid but couldn't hold it together. The day was a real mixture of emotions. The highlight was seeing all the family. I loved seeing my uncle, aunt and cousins – it was just a shame that Nan wasn't around to enjoy it!

Physically I was getting really big and people would make comments wherever I went, asking how long I had to go and was I excited? They were well meaning. Sometimes I just smiled and said we were expecting a girl and her due date was 17 September. Other times I told random strangers that she had Trisomy 18 and unless we had a miracle she wouldn't live. I had many opportunities to speak out my faith in the God of miracles and declare my trust in Him. Mark's mum, Helen, had found a magazine article by a couple in America whose Trisomy 18 baby Madeleine was now six and completely healed. Reading the story of their pregnancy was like a mirror image of ours. Helen had contacted Madeleine's parents and they were emailing us their support and encouragement. I was so excited to hear what God had done for them and it spurred me on to pray the same for Keziah.

Although Trisomy 18 isn't mentioned in the Bible, there is an incident in which a father, Jairus, cried out to Jesus on behalf of his daughter who was passing through the shadow of death. It's recorded in three of the Gospels. Jesus reassured Jairus, "Don't be afraid; just believe, and she will be healed" (Luke 8:50). And, indeed, she was. As I prayed, I would regularly speak these words over myself.

Since Keziah's due date was rapidly approaching, our hospital appointments were increasing. We had two final scans in August. As I mentioned before, these days were difficult. I thought often of something Bill Wilson had said, "In life, if you have the choice between taking the elevator and the stairs, always take the stairs." The elevator was the easy ride, the stairs would build muscle. This pregnancy was a climb up the stairs! Yet I felt it was a privilege to be entrusted with this upward climb as our spiritual muscles were definitely being developed. A favorite promise of God that I held onto confirmed this:

> The Lord God is my Strength, my personal bravery, and my invincible army; He makes my feet like hinds' feet and will make me walk [not to stand still in terror, but to walk] and make [spiritual] progress upon my high places [of trouble, suffering, or responsibility]!
>
> (Habbakuk 3:19 AMP)

I had many special moments along the journey when God showed me His kindness during the secret times of distress that only He saw.

At thirty-four weeks, during August, I had a scan during which the sonographer told me he couldn't see any sign of the cysts on Keziah's brain. It was the day after we had met to pray again and we had targeted each symptom, asking God to remove and heal. I was really excited that the cysts had dissolved but disappointed that the other symptoms were still there. The next morning Pastor Lydia sent me a beautiful text, through which I felt the kindness and grace of God again whispering His words of encouragement:

"I will not forget you!
See, I have engraved you on the palms of my hands;
your walls are ever before me."

(Isaiah 49:15-16)

Most of the time I was feeling strong in God and excited about what He was going to do.

I was enormous by now and pleased to be so big, thinking that Keziah was growing. I had my hospital bag packed and ready. Keziah's new little pink outfits were folded neatly alongside neutral-colored babygros from Josh's early days that were washed in preparation for her arrival. The Moses basket was also set up and ready in our bedroom. Alongside this expectancy with practical steps of faith, I also followed the pediatrician's advice by reading booklets about Trisomy 18 sent by SOFT (Support Organisation for Trisomy 18, 13 and Related Disorders).

One particular evening, I lay in the bath reading through the information. The more I read, the worse I felt. My thoughts began to wander down the unhelpful dark paths of the "What ifs?": "What if she's badly deformed?" "What if she's severely disabled, yet lives for years? How would that affect Josh?" Mark was out and only God witnessed my tears. I got out of the bath, staring at my enormous belly. Then, turning to the phone, I saw my friend Hayley had sent me a text message,

"Don't be afraid, for I am with you.
Don't be dismayed, for I am your God.

I will strengthen you and help you.
I will hold you up with my victorious right hand."
(Isaiah 41:10 NLT)

Immediately I silenced the "What ifs" and was comforted by God's promise. I knew I could trust Him, whatever the future held. He tells us to live for today and not to worry about tomorrow. For a few minutes I had forgotten His advice. When I spoke to Hayley later and told her how perfect the timing of her text had been, she simply said she'd been praying for me and couldn't get me out of her head. She knew God was prompting her to send the text message to me. Again I was touched by the kindness of God in hearing Hayley's prayer and comforting me by impressing upon her heart the need to obey, by reminding me of His promise. He would not fail me.

The following week we had our final scan. Unknown to us then, it was to be the last time we would see Keziah alive. Physically I had been feeling very nauseous. I was huge and uncomfortable. The scan showed the reason why. Keziah's stomach wasn't working properly so she wasn't swallowing the amniotic fluid. Polyhydramnios is a symptom of Trisomy 18. After the excitement of the cysts having disappeared at the last scan, this was such a disappointment. We were absolutely gutted. I just wanted to crawl into a corner, hide and cry. We came out of the scan room, tears flowing freely. I couldn't hold it together and didn't want to sit with all the other pregnant mums as we waited to see Miss Wright with the scan results. For a while I camped out in the woman's toilet until the tears stopped. When I'd composed myself, I re-joined Mark and together we were ushered through quickly to see Miss Wright. We were grateful again for Sarah Hartson's sensitivity and the way she handled us. Miss Wright, knowing all about Edwards babies, wasn't surprised at all by the excess fluid.

It hadn't been the best day of my life! Emotionally and physically I was exhausted; I couldn't seem to stop crying. I was thankful that these really bad days had been few and when they came, they took me by surprise.

When we got home, I cried again but this time they were good tears! I have been blessed with incredible friendships and I was continually being spoilt by those around me. On returning from hospital, two of my oldest school friends popped in to cheer me up. We had been friends now for over thirty years since primary school days. Lisa Lou always managed to make me laugh and Helen Mary blew me away that afternoon by her extravagant generosity and thoughtfulness. She and her husband, Samuel Lucas, arrived on the doorstep with a beautiful handcrafted bag overflowing with chocolate, sweets, flowers and a magazine. We're not talking a few bars – it looked as if they'd raided a factory. The confectionery supply kept Mark and me going for days!

Since my pregnancy with Josh, I'd collected a group of women friends (Jo, Joanne, Jenny, Abi and Serena) who all had children the same age. These women had been phenomenal, helping me out with childcare when willing grandparents weren't available. That afternoon they had taken Josh out for his friend's second birthday. Josh arrived back, having had a wonderful day out, and thankfully was oblivious to our pain. My parents also popped over to dish out much-needed hugs. When everyone had left, Mark sat at the piano and sang his song "Sing." The words gave me incredible comfort. As I listened to Mark worship, I sensed the presence of God in the room. I focused on all I had to be thankful for. The circumstances we were facing hadn't changed but I had. By that brief moment of re-focusing on God, my tears, recorded and stored up in heaven, had dried and "the peace of God, which transcends all understanding," as it says in Philippians 4:7, was back.

Chapter 10

NEARLY TIME...

"He who feeds on My flesh and drinks My blood dwells continually in Me, and I [in like manner dwell continually] in him."

(John 6:56 AMP)

With the arrival of September, Keziah's due date of the 17th was fast approaching. Mark's holiday was over and he was back in school full time. I had a final prayer time with the ladies and felt prepared for whatever was to happen. Josh's second birthday was imminent, on the 15th. I was hoping we could celebrate his special day and lavish him with love and affection before the arrival of his little sister. We had our final appointment with pediatrician Dr Turner, and his team had been informed that Keziah's arrival was pending. Although the circumstances were very different from Josh's arrival into the world, the excitement of finally meeting our unborn child was the same. I was thrilled that I had almost reached full term, giving Keziah every chance to grow and develop as much as was possible.

Josh's second birthday arrived, complete with a little party for a few of his friends. The daily fun and joy we had with Josh was such a gift and a huge blessing. Our final midwife appointment was scheduled for the following day. Since Miss Wright was away, we were seen by one of her colleagues. This was a little off-putting as we didn't really want to explain everything to someone new. In the end that wasn't necessary and the replacement obstetrician was charming and immediately put us at ease. I didn't want to be induced as I had been with Josh, so I was given a thorough sweep (apologies to my male readers!) and sent home with the expectancy that I would return later that day to the labor ward. Although I was in a lot of discomfort, there was no sign of labor starting.

Leaving Josh asleep with my parents, Mark and I went out for lunch together alone, thinking it would be the "last supper" before the birth. Unknown to us, we still had another week to go! The next few days I stayed quite close to home, expecting labor to start at any time. With everything we had been told, I hadn't thought Keziah would be overdue!

The following Tuesday, 23 September, I was up early with Josh as usual at 5 am. He had just had his second night out of the cot and in a big bed. By 7 am, both of us were ready to go back to bed. It was a slightly crazy timetable. I got into bed and lay down. Immediately I had a couple of sharp stabbing pains in my side and then stillness. Due to the excess fluid and Keziah's smallness, there was plenty of room for her to move around and it was normal to feel as if she was running her own aerobics class! This morning she was still. I prodded my tummy to encourage her to move but nothing happened. Fighting against the rising panic, I forced myself to stay calm, pray and wait. After thirty minutes had passed, I was in a dilemma. I still hadn't felt her move and even though it seemed like a lack of faith to even entertain thoughts that she had died, I wanted to be checked out. I phoned the hospital and explained the situation, and they told me to come straight in so they could examine me. Ironically, as soon as I put the phone down, I felt a big kick! I have never been so thankful to be kicked in all my life! Relief flooded through me that Keziah was still alive. I decided against ringing the hospital to say it had been a false alarm, so Mark and I turned up as expected, having dropped Josh off at my parents on the way. I had my hospital bag with me just in case they decided to keep me in for monitoring. When we arrived at the hospital, they listened to Keziah's heartbeat and measured my tummy. I was forty-seven inches in diameter! How funny! I resembled a perfect forty-seven-inch round beach ball. I was given a second thorough sweep by a nutty junior doctor. She made me laugh by discarding any formalities, telling me not to be embarrassed as I was the eighteenth vagina she had seen that morning! A little humor always helps!

We left the hospital sure that this would kick-start Keziah's arrival and went to collect Josh. We all went out to lunch together and then, when we got home, I spent the afternoon asleep. I wanted to rest as much as possible. That afternoon, I took communion by myself as I had done the afternoon before Josh's birth. John 6:56 (quoted at the beginning of the chapter) had powerfully ministered to me two years previously as I'd prepared myself for Josh's labor and I wanted to do the same for Keziah's. As I took the bread and ribena (I didn't have a bottle of red wine open!), I loved the fact that the reality of Jesus was closer to me than my breath. Totally amazing! What comfort, help and reassurance.

At 9.30 pm I began to experience strange recurring pains. They didn't feel like contractions but I knew something was happening. I couldn't lie down flat or stand up straight and was only comfortable bending forward or resting on the birthing ball. It was going to be a long night. This was it! We had a plan in place for this moment. We called my friend Helen Mary and asked her to come over. Under normal circumstances I knew it was best to stay at home for as long as possible but, in case of emergency, I wanted to be at the hospital where help was readily at hand. Helen Mary was here within two minutes. We called the hospital and told them I was coming in. I knew there was a chance they would send me home until labor had progressed a little further, but my bag came with me just in case! It seemed a bit surreal that this moment had actually arrived.

Chapter 11

THE BIRTH

⌇

*He who dwells in the secret place of the Most High shall
remain stable and fixed under the shadow of the Almighty
[Whose power no foe can withstand]. I will say of the Lord,
He is my Refuge and my Fortress, my God; on Him I lean and
rely, and in Him I [confidently] trust!*

(Psalm 91:1-2 AMP)

The journey to the hospital was pretty uncomfortable as
I couldn't sit properly in the front seat of the car. Thankfully, at this time of night there was no traffic and we arrived
within a few minutes. The car park and foyer were eerily quiet, unlike the normal daytime hustle and bustle. I wondered
fleetingly if the next time I exited the hospital doors, Keziah
would be in my arms. The labor ward were expecting us,
and we were met by a lovely Ghanaian midwife called
Ophelia. (We found out later that she was a Christian and
she sat and prayed with us before her shift ended.) She
listened to Keziah's heartbeat, which was strong, and monitored me, deciding that contractions had started but, due
to all the excess fluid, I was feeling them in a strange place.
I was given the choice to go home and return when contractions were stronger and more regular, or remain and wait it out.

I decided to stay. The minutes were passing slowly. I made myself as comfortable as I could on a big blue inflatable as I still couldn't lie flat on the bed. Mark made the most of this opportunity and took residence on the empty bed, remaining there until daylight, his intermittent snoring keeping me company! Fortunately, over in Hong Kong where my brother Andrew lives, it was the middle of the day. He was a fantastic long-distance support, phoning and texting me encouragement throughout the night.

By the time Ophelia went off shift at 7 am, I was starting to take gas and air (entonox) as the contractions were now about five minutes apart. A new midwife called Caroline was assigned to us. She recognized us and, after looking in our notes, realized that she had been the training midwife in the room when Josh was born two years previously. This certainly hadn't happened just by chance. We were sure God had handpicked her to be with us. She was the perfect choice. She and her fellow midwife Tania never left us alone until after Keziah had arrived. They were absolutely fantastic. Every fifteen minutes, Caroline monitored Keziah's heartbeat. Throughout the labor it remained strong and steady, showing no signs of distress.

My parents arrived at around 8 am. Dad took Mark out for breakfast to build him up for the day ahead and Mum remained with me. Back at home, Helen Mary had completed the night shift with Josh and gone off to work. Grandma Helen had taken over, so we knew Josh was having a whale of a time with the two Helens! By this time, I was 5 cm dilated and Caroline estimated that the cervix should continue to dilate about 1 cm per hour, putting Keziah's arrival somewhere between 2 and 3 pm. This really was it: the final countdown until we would meet her.

Over the next few hours, things started to heat up and the contractions were becoming longer and stronger. I was concentrating on my breathing and as I used the entonox, with each contraction, I was focusing on a different promise of God. I was really conscious of His presence surrounding me in every way. Although the room was filling up with different doctors preparing for Keziah's arrival, I really felt that God had tucked me tight under the shadow of His wing as described in Psalm 17:

Show the wonder of your great love,
you who save by your right hand
those who take refuge in you from their foes.
Keep me as the apple of your eye;
hide me in the shadow of your wings.

(vv. 7-8)

By the time the waters were broken around midday, the pain was so intense that the next two hours are slightly hazy in my memory. As a result of the amount of gas I was inhaling I was totally away with the fairies. Amidst the intensity of the situation, my delirious state was a source of amusement to myself, Mark and Mum. I was coming out with some crazy stuff! I could see Mark and Mum trying to hide their smiles, not wanting to upset me. I was very happy to be delirious, not minding their amusement, as long as the pain was kept at bay!

The last part of the labor was horrendous. I didn't know until afterwards that Keziah had turned into a posterior position which was far from ideal for birth. Her back was against my back. She had got stuck. Caroline didn't tell me at the time in case I gave up trying to deliver her myself. I did wonder more than once during this time why I hadn't insisted on a caesarean section. We had discussed this during our appointments with Miss Wright, but we had arrived at the conclusion that it was best for me to go for as natural a delivery as possible so that I wouldn't have the additional problems of recovering from an operation myself. In that way, straight after the birth,

I would be as mobile as possible in order to care for both Josh and Keziah. In hindsight that was certainly the best decision, but for a split second when I didn't know if I could continue, I did doubt its wisdom. I was utterly exhausted and my legs were shaking uncontrollably. Caroline and Tania were absolutely amazing, telling me what to do to guide Keziah out. They called the doctor and said that as I'd been pushing for forty-five minutes, they would need him to intervene. That scared me into action and spurred me on to do it myself! Somehow, I managed to push the right way and next thing I knew at 1.57 pm, Wednesday 24 September 2008, Keziah Esther Joy Grayson was born.

Mark cut her cord and I kept asking, "Is she alive? Is she alive?" "Come on, Kezzie! Come on, Kezzie!" I urged. The whole room was completely silent. No one said anything. Mum started crying, then Mark. I knew then she hadn't made it.

Chapter 12

ONE NIGHT IN A LIFETIME

He will cover you with his feathers,
and under his wings you will find refuge;
his faithfulness will be your shield and rampart.

(Psalm 91:4)

I was stunned. I don't think that it registered straight away that she wasn't alive. For a brief moment I was in shock. After all that pain and effort, she hadn't made it. Even with all that we had been told, I just hadn't expected that. I didn't believe she was going to die. Her strong heartbeat throughout labor had given me no indication that her little heart wouldn't hold out for the final push. It was quite surreal.

She was taken immediately over to a waiting incubator and quietly examined before being wrapped in a little white towel and given to me to hold, a precious little bundle. Her tiny body was still warm. She was so beautiful: a miniature, feminine, delicate version of Josh but with loads of dark hair. Her eyes were closed but her tiny light-pink rosebud lips were slightly open. Apart from her right ear looking a little abnormal and a couple of overlapping fingers, externally she looked so perfect. Her legs were long with a gorgeous pair of little feet on the end. Contrary to the indications of the scan, both arms looked the same length. She was like a delicate little china doll. Apart from the stillness of her chest, she just looked as if she was asleep. I expected her to open her eyes suddenly, screw her face up and announce her arrival into the world with a loud cry, yet it never came. She was born to heaven and had bypassed this world from my womb straight into the arms of her creator, my God.

Mark held her and my heart broke to see him hold his little princess in his arms. He just gazed at her, studying her intently, wanting to absorb every detail. He looked so proud to be her daddy. Nestled in his arms, with the top of her head poking out of the towel, it looked like any normal scene played out on the labor ward, but this wasn't normal. Instead of being the start of her life on earth, it was the end of her time with us physically, yet the beginning of her life in a different realm. From the moment of her conception, she was a tiny being, a life formed in my womb. God had entrusted her to us, and although her time with us was so short, it had been incredibly special. We were now a family of four – she had just gone before us.

After her grandparents had had a chance to hold her, she was then passed back to Caroline and Tania. They carefully wiped her down and recorded her length and weight; they took prints of her hand and feet and a lock of her hair for us to treasure and keep. We had chosen to dress her in a little pink and white dress and cardigan that her Aunty Helen Mary had bought, complete with a little nappy and pink knickers. We had bought a soft pink fleecy blanket, which she was carefully wrapped in. Mark filmed everything that was happening as I was stuck on the bed. Due to a problem with my placenta, which was thankfully resolved soon after, I wasn't allowed to move. Miraculously, I didn't need stitches and there was not a single tear. I had to remain on the bed for several hours following her birth with a drip in to stop any hemorrhaging. I found that incredibly frustrating as

I couldn't quite see what they were doing with Keziah, even though they were only about a meter and a half away from me. Mark kept filming and an abundance of photos were taken so that as far as possible every detail was captured. Again, everything seemed so surreal. I wasn't sure whether to smile or cry in the photos.

I was completely heartbroken. Yet at the same time I wanted to enjoy the tangible softness of her skin and soak up every detail of her sweet face. I couldn't stop stroking her cheeks: they were incredibly soft to touch. We just spent time holding her, loving her, talking to her and enjoying this precious time with her little body in our arms.

We had decided that if she didn't survive the birth, then it wouldn't be appropriate to bring Josh in to meet her. It would have been too traumatic and bewildering for him to see us crying one minute and smiling the next as we alternated between the grief of her loss and the wonder of her being. Both sets of our parents and Mark's brother Phil had been taking turns in keeping Josh amused on the hospital premises but we didn't bring him onto the labor ward. That night, our only night with Keziah, would ironically be the longest time in Josh's life that I had ever been apart from him. As they all said goodbye to leave us with Keziah, Mark also left to return home briefly and shower. Helen Mary came in to help me get washed and refreshed.

We placed Kezzie in a little cot. She looked so peaceful and serene, all snugly wrapped up. I was reluctant to leave her side for even a moment. I wanted time to stand still. I just kept studying her, wanting to memorize every little detail of her face and etch it on my memory so that I would never forget. I still couldn't quite grasp that she wasn't alive. With everyone out of the room, Helen Mary and I held hands and prayed. I laid hands on Keziah and prayed that the same spirit that raised Jesus from the dead, that lives in me, would raise her from the dead and give life to her mortal

body through His Spirit (Romans 8:11). It was a scripture I
had spoken over her while she was in my womb. I knew that
God was able to do the impossible. A truth ingrained in my
heart, that I refused to let go, was Jesus' statement in Mark
10:27: "all things are possible with God." I believed it. As I
prayed, I expected her eyelids to blink, her chest to move
and her lips to breathe.

Later that evening when Mark returned, we prayed over
her again. It was only when we finally said goodbye the following morning that I knew that, for whatever reason, I wouldn't
see the miracle of Keziah being brought back to life. When I
mentioned to Mark that Lazarus had been dead and buried
as recorded in John 11, he said he didn't think that would
happen here. Maybe I was totally crazy but my reasoning
was if Jesus did it once and He's the same yesterday, today
and forever (Hebrews 13:8), then it was pretty simple for
Him to do it again!

Sarah Hartson came by to see us and meet Keziah. Then
we were moved from the labor ward to a special suite called
the "Sands" room which was sensitively situated, around the
corner, tucked away from the other newborns in the maternity ward. By this time I was completely exhausted and
feeling extremely nauseous from the physical effort of the
labor and all the emotion surrounding her birth. By 7.45 pm,
we had turned out the lights and were snuggled up on the
bed when Caroline knocked on the door with some official
forms for us to sign. We had to make a few decisions regard-
ing what would happen with her body. During the whole of
the pregnancy it had never crossed my mind that we would
have to arrange her funeral. It seemed such an alien concept
to link with a newborn, yet I had to keep reminding myself
that she was stillborn and not newborn, so these were decisions we would have to make.

We eventually fell asleep with Keziah in the cot beside
our bed. I was reluctant to shut my eyes as I wanted to

stay awake all night looking at her. I didn't want to waste one second of our time with her, our only night together. With each second that passed, I was conscious that it was getting closer to the time when we would have to say our final goodbye and walk out of the room, leaving her body behind. While I knew her body was just a shell and that life had left her, nevertheless her body represented her. Physical changes were already slowly taking place as her lips were becoming a darker red and her skin although still soft was no longer warm to touch. It was unbearably hot in the room and I woke up at midnight needing water and some painkillers. Mark was also awake, so we listened to the Aerosmith song "I don't want to miss a thing" on the Ipod. The words were incredibly apt and tears were just streaming freely down our faces. An amusing incident then broke the intensity of the moment as a couple of midwives knocked on the door to give me some painkillers. Since Mark hadn't bought anything to sleep in, he was sitting on the sofa in the corner, by Keziah in her cot, with nothing on except a cushion! That did make me chuckle! At 2 am we eventually turned the light out again and managed to sleep until morning.

Mark was up first and went off to feed the parking meter and bring us back breakfast. I got myself ready and thanked God that my body had seemed to bounce back. It certainly didn't feel as if I had survived such a horrendous labor less than twenty-four hours previously. Our Pastors, Alan and Lydia, arrived about 9.45 and we spent a lovely hour talking with them. Lydia shared some scriptures and Alan prayed, all the while with Keziah in the cot beside us.

After they had left, I bumped into the ceramics lady on the maternity ward and I asked her if she would come and print Keziah's foot in clay for us. She was very hesitant but agreed to do so since I was so calm. I was really grateful she agreed as I could see she felt really awkward, yet I knew it would be such a precious, special memory.

As midday approached, we were aware that soon we would have to say our final goodbyes and walk out of the door, leaving Keziah's body behind us. I sat by the side of her cot, drinking in the side view of her beautiful little face. We took hundreds of snaps from all different angles. My cousin Simon had dropped off a beautiful bouquet of yellow flowers with my favorite gerberas included, so I put one by the side of her face.

To walk away from her body that day was one of the hardest things I've ever had to do. It was heartbreaking that the time had come to leave her behind. We kissed her so many times before we finally summoned the courage to say goodbye and leave her physical body lying there looking so peaceful. We said one final prayer, asking God to help us leave her behind and thanking Him for the gift of Josh. Knowing that we were going to pick Josh up gave us the strength to walk out of the door.

It seemed strange to be leaving the maternity ward empty handed and several times I had to resist the urge to turn around and run back to Keziah, sweep her up in my arms and cuddle her one more time. A midwife accompanied us out of the door of the labor ward and we literally bumped straight into Keziah's pediatrician, Dr Craig Turner. God's timing was so perfect. Dr Turner went out of his way to walk us out of the hospital doors. It was another lovely caring touch from fantastic hospital staff. We were conscious that we had been given extraordinary treatment by all the professionals involved. Dr Turner's parting words were a comfort at the right time. He said that from the moment he had met us he had been struck by our faith and courage.

He added that the way I carried myself was the reason that Keziah hadn't shown any distress during labor. His kind words made me cry and I thanked God. I knew it wasn't me – it was the wonderful gift of His presence with me. I felt totally helpless: all I could do was lean on the Eternal One who loved me.

Chapter 13

"HE BORE MY GRIEF AND CARRIED MY PAIN"

The Lord is a refuge for the oppressed,
a stronghold in times of trouble.
Those who know your name will trust in you,
for you, Lord, have never forsaken those who seek you.
(Psalm 9:9-10)

Josh was so excited to see us when we arrived at my parents' house. He kept planting little kisses on our knees, running off, then coming back and kissing us again. When we got back to our house, the first of many gorgeous bouquets had been delivered. I had sent a text out in the middle of the night on Wednesday when we were in the Sands room. It seemed an easy way to inform people. We played with Josh, gave him tea, prayed with him and put him to bed. That evening Mark and I wrote up Keziah's birth on the Caring Bridge website and added some of our favorite photos. I still couldn't believe she wasn't there with us.

I woke up several times that night and immediately realized something felt different. I realized with a start that for so long I had been used to feeling Keziah moving inside me.

It then hit me that she had been born and now she was gone. The emptiness and sense of loss were unbearable. It was natural that my womb would now be empty but the physical ache of having empty arms, with no baby to cuddle, was a new pain I had to handle. Once again the nocturnal whisper of the Holy Spirit spoke to my heart. Isaiah 53:4 says: "Surely he hath borne our griefs, and carried our sorrows" (KJV). Jesus, my Savior, had suffered unbearably on the cross so that I didn't have to. "He bore my griefs and carried my pain" was a truth I repeated to myself constantly, speaking it out loud many times over the next few months.

I could get through this if I kept clinging to Him. The sense of loss was like a huge gaping hole in my heart, yet I wasn't alone. Jesus identified with my pain and my grief. The divine exchange that took place at the cross was at the heart of my faith. He was made sin with my sinfulness so that I could be made righteous with His righteousness (paraphrase of 2 Corinthians 5:21). Jesus took the rubbish for me and in its place gave me His perfect, beautiful righteousness, so that my relationship with God could be restored. I knew that because of the cross there was a way forward for me. Even though the pain cut so deep, I knew it was possible to walk in victory through this time.

Another one of my favorite truths stood out to me, emphasizing the reality of Christ's victory on the cross and what that provided for me.

> For if, by the trespass of the one man, death reigned through that one man, how much more will those who receive God's abundant provision of grace and of the gift of righteousness reign in life through the one man, Jesus Christ.
>
> (Romans 5:17)

The provision was there for me, waiting and available. Provision that meant that, even in my loss and grief, I could reign during this season of my life. I knew that if I just kept taking my grief and my pain to the cross, Jesus would bring healing to my heart and make me whole again. I liked the way the Amplified Bible explained it in Isaiah 53:5:

But He was wounded for our transgressions, He was bruised for our guilt and iniquities; the chastisement [needful to obtain] peace and well-being for us was upon Him, and with the stripes [that wounded] Him we are healed and made whole.

Peace, well-being, healing and wholeness, I needed all of those. I carried the peace of God within me as a benefit of my salvation. From the pain of losing Keziah, I would need to push into God until my heart was healed and whole again. Hope was there, like an anchor.

I didn't realize the amount of practicalities that came with a death. The next morning Mark had to phone up the funeral director's. It felt like an arrow in my heart hearing him say it was for his daughter. There was no charge for Keziah's funeral, which I thought was a beautiful act of kindness to help soothe the pain.* Throughout the morning, bouquets of flowers kept arriving, along with a pile of cards. My friend Caitlin came over to collect Josh to play with her boys for the afternoon. Mark went out to order prints of all the photos we had taken of Keziah as I had such a longing to see her little face. While everyone was out and I was on my own, I watched the video of Keziah's birth. Mark had actually filmed her coming out. I had one particular song called the "Desert Song" from the Hillsong album *This is our God* on repeat in my ear. The song was written by a lady who had given birth at twenty weeks to her first child who had died. The words were so powerful because they were a declaration of victory without

---

* This is true of the larger undertakers. Some smaller family companies do make a small charge to cover the cost.

denying the pain. They strengthened me as I sat there, tears streaming down my face.

This is my prayer in the desert
When all that's within me feels dry.
This is my prayer in my hunger and need,
My God is the God who provides.

And this is my prayer in the fire,
Through weakness, or trial, or pain.
There is a faith proved
Of more worth than gold,
So refine me Lord, through the flame.

I will bring praise, I will bring praise,
No weapon formed against me shall remain.
I will rejoice,
I will declare,
God is my victory and He is here.

This is my prayer in the battle,
When triumph is still on its way.
I am a conqueror, co-heir with Christ,
So firm on His promise I'll stand.

All of my life,
In every season,
You are still God,
I have a reason to sing.
I have a reason to worship.

This is my prayer in the harvest
When favor and providence flow.
I know I'm filled to be emptied again.
The seed I've received I will sow.

I cried and cried, giving a release to my pain. I still couldn't believe she was gone. The pain of losing her had broken something deep inside me. I felt so fragile and vulnerable, yet sensed that God was holding me gently in the palm of His hand like a delicate treasure. The tears would not stop and in those first few days immediately after the birth, whenever I was alone in the house, I let them flow and flow.

The next morning, now three days after the birth, I had another problem to deal with – one I hadn't given much thought to before. I had fed Josh myself for almost six months after his birth. My body now wanted to do the same for Keziah but there was no outlet. All I could do was sit it out, take painkillers, stuff cold savoy cabbage leaves in my bra (yes, seriously!) and wait for relief to come! My friend Jo came round to collect Josh to play with her sons Harry and Lucas, two of Josh's little friends, so we could once again have a few hours alone to grieve and sort stuff out. Mark went out to pick up the photos of Keziah. I slept, then eagerly waited for him to return. I was so desperate to see the photos and have a picture of her face in front of me to look at. Even though I knew she was safe in heaven and completely perfect, I guess my body was wondering where the baby I'd given birth to had gone. I wanted something tangible to hold.

In the months to come I spent hours looking at the photos over and over again. I was so pleased we had taken so many of our brief time with her.

We didn't go to church that first Sunday after the birth. Pastors Alan and Lydia read out a statement that Mark had written explaining our journey since 1 May. Many people in church hadn't known about the Trisomy 18 and would have expected to see us with a newborn. I felt such a heaviness that day that I knew I didn't want to live under, so Monday morning I got up prepared to fight. I was determined to shake off and chase away the despair that was trying to worm its way in. I prayed in tongues for ages and just sang in the Spirit. I read out loud lots of my favorite scriptures and I kept saying, "You bore my grief and carried my pain, Jesus, so I don't have to." I was determined to do what it says in Hebrews 13:15,

> Through Jesus, therefore, let us continually offer to God a sacrifice of praise – the fruit of lips that confess his name.

While Mark was still asleep, I put on one of Josh's children's praise DVDs and Josh and I danced around the room, singing the Hillsong "Number One" song,

> I won't stop,
> Never gonna stop praising,
> Every day You'll be my number one,
> Jesus! Jesus!
> My number one!

I swung Josh round, enjoying his infectious laughter, and worshiped and sang until I had pushed through the heaviness into His presence. I knew if I could succeed just once I would set myself a mandate for the days to come. I ignored my feelings and disciplined myself to praise and there I got my breakthrough! I got the peace and the joy of God right in my heart. Psalm 16:11 declares,

> You have made known to me the path of life;
> you will fill me with joy in your presence,
> with eternal pleasures at your right hand.

I had shaken off the heaviness and was ready to face the day ahead: I took the first step and the Holy Spirit then partnered with me, bringing me through to victory. This was my daily sacrifice of praise. God honored and accepted it.

Chapter 14

A TIME TO MOURN

There is a time for everything,
and a season for every activity under heaven:
a time to be born and a time to die...
a time to weep and a time to laugh,
a time to mourn...

(Ecclesiastes 3:1, 3-4)

We had a busy day ahead. We had booked to go to a hotel in Bournemouth the next day for a few days' break, so there was a list of practical jobs that needed to be done in preparation for the funeral the following Tuesday. Together we planned the order of service and Mark formatted it beautifully. We ordered the food for after the funeral, then dropped Josh off with his grandparents so we could go to the registry office alone. It was a strange experience to register the birth and the death at the same time. We then took the order of service to the printer's, leaving it there to be collected later. In the meantime, we went hunting for two identical little teddies. We wanted to put one in the casket to be cremated with Keziah and one to go in her keepsake box for us. We found two adorable floppy pink and white bunnies. At times it seemed as if we were acting out parts in a play and we would soon step out of this surreal world and back into normal life. I was taking painkillers every four hours to numb the headache that had been constant since Keziah's birth. My body was still adjusting to having no baby to hold. I felt exhausted from all the jobs we were squeezing into the day.

As we walked around the shopping center, I kept looking at different people, wondering what was going on in their worlds. I'm sure we didn't look like a couple who were busy arranging their daughter's funeral. I wondered what other tragedies were hidden behind the outward appearances of normalcy. With no baby to stop and cuddle and rest with, I think I kept forgetting that I had given birth only five days previously. I sat and rested while Mark returned to the printer's to collect the order of service.

Our next stop was at the florist's to order the funeral flowers. I wanted all the women who were coming to hold a single pink gerbera, and the men a single white one. We chose a simple posy of pink and white gerberas to sit on top of the casket. Our final stop of the day was at Pastors Alan and Lydia's house to go through what we had decided on for the funeral. Alan would conduct the service and we wanted Lydia, along with the other senior leaders, to read out scriptures that had been particularly special to us throughout the pregnancy. We thought it was too much to ask the grandparents to read and I knew I wouldn't be up for the task. We included Mark's song "Sing" in the order and several of the worship songs I had played throughout the pregnancy to begin and end the service. We were exhausted by the time we picked up Josh and put him to bed. We gratefully received a wonderful meal cooked for us by a friend, Maxene, from church and collapsed gladly into bed soon after.

The following morning, Mark took the bunny we had bought over to the funeral director's while I packed our bags and tidied the house ready for our departure. It rained the entire journey. When we arrived at the hotel mid-afternoon, the weather was so gloomy. The hotel stank of fish and we were the youngest guests by about fifty years! Our room was pretty dated, and I sat there and wanted to cry. I knew it was crazy, but I felt as if we had abandoned Keziah by coming away. It seemed like a mad idea that we had come. We both decided it was too late to think like that and we needed to change our attitudes and make the most of our time together. I kept thinking that this time last week Keziah was still alive in my womb. Not even a week had passed, yet it seemed as if we had lived several decades in those few days. In one sense, I wanted to hide away with Mark and Josh. I was safe in their company. I didn't have to explain anything.

It actually turned out to be a special few days together. The first evening Mark took Josh swimming and it was so beautiful watching the sheer delight on Josh's face as he splashed around. He absolutely loves the water. We then went out exploring the area in the car and ended up having dinner out. Josh was hilarious. He must have realized it was a treat to be out so late, because he certainly made the most of it! He was determined to capture the attention of every-one in the restaurant and spent the entire evening waving, smiling and pulling faces at his audience. It felt good to have a light respite between the trauma of the past week and the upcoming funeral.

The next morning, the contrast in the weather was like a personal gift from God! It was magnificent. Gone were the rain and gloom, and in their place was a glorious clear blue sky resplendent with bright autumn sunshine. The air was crisp and fresh, and we wandered along the seafront breath-ing in deeply! I had hardly slept during the night and Josh was wide awake at 4.45 am, so by 9.30 am we were shattered and back in bed. The three of us slept soundly until midday.

It was bliss! We spent the afternoon exploring a National Trust property in the local area, then I left the boys back at the hotel while I went hunting for something to wear for the funeral. I wanted to wear baby pink, which wasn't a color I had in my wardrobe. I didn't want to wear black or grey. It was really important to me that I had something special to wear as, apart from the Thanksgiving service a few months later, there would be no other special occasions from her life that we would be able to celebrate. I eventually bought a baby-pink soft pashmina to wear over white trousers and a long beige top.

Mark had told me that he wanted to carry Keziah for the funeral. He didn't want a stranger doing it. His reasoning was that he would never have the chance to walk her down the aisle on her wedding day, so at the crematorium he would honor her life now by carrying her tiny casket to the front, ready for the committal.

The following day we returned home. I had a migraine, so slept for most of the journey. We stopped off halfway, in Winchester, to visit Ken and Gloria, close friends of Mark's family. Their hospitality was extravagant and they lavished us with love. We left clutching an enormous, exquisite bouquet of pink and white roses, having been prayed for, comforted, strengthened and hugged! I found it really upsetting arriving home again, as if the little break away had been a way of escaping what had really happened. There was another huge pile of cards waiting for us plus more flowers. Kew Gardens now didn't have a patch on our household display of floral splendor!

The following evening, Friday 5 October, now nine days after Keziah's birth, we had a women's conference at church. It was the first time I was to walk back into church and face people. I felt terribly fragile and vulnerable, yet at the same time very conscious of God carrying me close. I had kindly been reserved a seat on the front row and I had an escort of my favorite women surrounding me so that I wasn't approached by too many well-meaning ladies. The ones I was close to, my entourage vetted and allowed to come near – it was quite funny watching them. I was amused and touched by their kindness and thankful for the way they were carefully protecting me. One of my best friends, Van, who is a South African, had strategically placed herself diagonally to my right so I could rely on an encouraging smile and get support if I was faltering.

I love the power of corporate worship in church, and as I lifted my hands in praise that first evening back in the house of God, I identified with a passage of Bill Johnson's book that I had read very recently:

Isaiah 60:18 says, "But you shall call your walls Salvation, and your gates Praise." In Revelation we see this gate called praise again and discover that it is made out of one solid pearl (see Rev. 21:21). Think for a moment. How is a pearl formed? Through irritation and conflict. A granule of sand gets inside an oyster shell, and a pearl forms around the granule to keep it from doing harm. The Bible's pairing of praise with irritation is not coincidental. When we are stuck in conflict and uncertainty, and yet we praise Him without manipulation, it is a sacrifice. It means we are reacting in a way that produces something beautiful. In that moment a gate is formed, a place of entrance where the King of glory can invade our situation... Psalm 87:2 says, "The Lord loves the gates of Zion more than all the dwellings of Jacob." That gate – that place of praise in the midst of conflict – is where His presence rests, where the King Himself dwells. The gate is formed when we move above human explanation and into a place of trust.

(*The Supernatural Power of a Transformed Mind*, p. 122)

As I worshiped that night, feeling so incredibly vulnerable, I felt the Holy Spirit say that as we chose to praise God still, despite Keziah's death, we reacted in a way that produced something beautiful. We hadn't blamed God; we hadn't got angry with Him. We had chosen to love Him, to trust Him and to praise Him through it, knowing that He is good and for us, all the time. Because we had done this, our gate had been formed, the place of entrance where the King of Glory could come and invade our situation.

We didn't know why Keziah had not been healed, as we knew God was well able; nevertheless, our lack of understanding did not take away our trust in the Almighty God who loves us. Because of this new glimpse of His character and the tenderness I sensed from Him, I knew it was a privilege to have gone through our suffering. We had nowhere else to turn anyway. As Simon Peter says in John 6:68-9,

> "Lord, to whom shall we go? You have the words of eternal life. We believe and know that you are the Holy One of God."

Chapter 15

THE FUNERAL

Turn your ear to me, come quickly to my rescue;
be my rock of refuge, a strong fortress to save me.
Since you are my rock and my fortress,
for the sake of your name lead and guide me.

(Psalm 31:2-3)

It was perfect timing to have the women's conference the weekend just before the funeral. I was lovingly chaperoned to and from the church so that I wasn't left alone. Fru, a friend from church, escorted me on the Saturday. She arrived to pick me up armed with a huge box of her delicious homemade flapjacks. She had made me a batch the week Josh was born, two years previously, and I had enjoyed them so much I had cheekily put in a request for Keziah's arrival. I now associate Fru's flapjacks with the two births of our children! Simple acts of kindness such as these touched me very deeply. My emotions felt so raw, like a huge gaping wound exposed for all to view. Everything felt tender and sore, yet the love I was experiencing from those around me was so beautiful, like a glimpse of sunlight on an otherwise cloudy day. The conference kept me occupied, and Mark and Josh enjoyed some special time together.

The funeral was scheduled for the following Tuesday at 12 o'clock. We had only invited our immediate family and leaders from church, intending at some later date to have a thanksgiving service, to which everyone could come. We needed to get the house ready for inviting everyone back afterwards. One of my mum's friends, Pearl, arrived on the Monday morning and did an amazing job of transforming the house while I shopped for thankyou presents for our midwives. They had been so phenomenal throughout the birth we wanted to bless them and show our appreciation. That afternoon I had an interesting encounter in the shopping center with a lady that used to bring her child to Shake, Rattle and Rollover. She saw me choosing baby clothes for the daughter of our main midwife, Caroline, and, glancing at my post-birth belly, wrongly assumed I was shopping for our child. I'd had two similar incidents the previous week in Bournemouth where women had wished me all the best for the coming birth! When I calmly explained that I had already had the baby and she died, they got more upset than I did! I forgot that we had lived with the whole scenario since 1 May and had adapted to it. For others, it was a complete shock and women especially empathized, knowing it could well have happened to them. I did find it quite exhausting when confronted with other people's reactions and grief. I suppose the majority of time immediately following the birth I did most of my grieving in private and tried to hold it together in public. It wasn't always possible and certainly wouldn't be during the funeral, but I used to sense God's peace rest on me, strengthening me when it was necessary to explain our circumstances.

Tears of gratitude seemed to come very readily during this time as I was touched by the way friends and family went out of their way to do something special for us. Books were left on our doorstep, CDs pushed through the door, plants given in Keziah's memory and monetary gifts given to bless and encourage us. The mums of Josh's friends even clubbed together to buy us a star which they named after Keziah. It made me think of Isaiah 40:26:

Lift your eyes and look to the heavens;
Who created all these?
He who brings out the starry host one by one,
and calls them each by name.

We felt very loved. On returning from my shopping trip that Monday, I found Judi had popped over with a glorious winter pansy array for the chimney pot on our front doorstep. She had also left by the front door two huge pots resplendent with beautiful burnt-orange and yellow autumnal floral displays. I was so touched.

The morning of the funeral arrived. I'd been reading through the Bible each year for a long time now and it seemed very appropriate that this particular morning I happened to be in Psalm 31 and 32. David had written both psalms during a time of trouble in his life. I identified with his emotions and was grateful for his honest account of events. He didn't hide or deny his pain, yet he always pointed back to the unchanging character of God. Once again, his decision to concentrate on the love and strength of God helped me to focus:

I will be glad and rejoice in your love,
for you saw my affliction
and knew the anguish of my soul.

(Psalm 31:7)

For a split second that morning, I felt like running away. I didn't want to face the funeral of our little daughter.

I didn't want to think of her still body, by now cold and hard to touch, lying alone in a box. I didn't want to stare at her tiny casket and watch it disappear forever.

I knew these weren't helpful thoughts, so I let them pass
through my mind rather than indulging them and letting
them dwell. I knew that was just her physical earthly body
and I believed she had a new, beautiful, perfect body, free
to run around and enjoy heaven. Nevertheless, right then
I was very conscious that we were on earth without her.
I turned my attention back to the Psalms and found immediate comfort in the following verses of Psalm 32:

> Therefore, let everyone who is godly pray to you
> while you may be found;
> surely when the mighty waters rise,
> they will not reach him.
> You are my hiding-place;
> you will protect me from trouble
> and surround me with songs of deliverance...
> the Lord's unfailing love surrounds the man
> who trusts in him.
>
> (vv. 6, 7, 10)

God had helped me so far. I knew that today He would give
me the strength I needed. It was time to get up and face the
day ahead.

Mark arrived back from dropping Josh round at Jo's for the
morning, followed by Helen Mary and Samuel Lucas with
the last few catering essentials we needed. They'd helped
us prepare the kitchen the previous evening. Judi and Van
were picking up the food in our absence, so all was now set.
We were ready to go. It's funny the details that stand out in
your memory during times of intense emotion. I remember
thinking the weather was perfect for the day. The sky was
blue and sun bright, yet there was a chill in the air, appropriate for October. While the bright sun matched the hope
we had that Keziah was safe in the arms of God and that

one day we would be reunited with her, the chill seemed to match our grief that it didn't quite seem natural that we were attending her funeral.

On the way we picked up the individual gerberas, ready to be handed out along with the orders of service, and were the first to arrive at the crematorium. Mark and I wanted to arrive before anyone else to have the time and space to think about the coming service.

My sister Nicky had traveled up from Devon and I sat with her, Mum and Dad as we waited for the service to begin. I will never forget Mark's face as he stood in the foyer holding Keziah's little white casket, trying to compose himself to walk her down the aisle. Tearstained and crumbled with grief, it was heart wrenching to watch, a Daddy's private moment holding his daughter, waiting to bury her along with his dreams for her life. I was so proud of him that he had the courage to do it. I know it was a defining moment of his life.

Pastor Alan led the service and spoke very eloquently of the hope we have in Jesus: the hope that one day we will see Keziah and be reunited with her. When that time comes, there will be no sickness, no Trisomy 18, no death.

Pastor Lydia read out the verses in the Bible relating to Keziah's names, and our other church leaders and friends, Pastor Mark Wiltshire, Deborah and Rob, read some of our favorite scriptures, which we had spoken regularly over Keziah while she was alive in my womb. It was unbearable to watch the casket slowly descend downwards during the committal. It seemed so final. She really had gone. The last words that Deborah read from the front just before the coffin was lowered were from my favorite truth in Scripture,

The Lord your God is with you,
he is mighty to save.

He will take great delight in you,
he will quiet you with his love,
he will rejoice over you with singing.

(Zephaniah 3:17)

Even though I was shaking and crying uncontrollably as I
watched the coffin disappear, the words "he will quiet you
with his love" were going round and round in my head.
I knew that not only would God quiet me with His love,
He was able to do the same for Keziah. Physically we may
have been separated, but there is no distance in the spirit. I,
like Keziah, was God's daughter and I felt comforted by my
Heavenly Father's love. The fact He held us both in safety,
bought comfort to my soul.

Although the entire service lasted only about ten minutes,
the intensity of emotion made it seem as if we had been there
for hours. Grief was draining and physically exhausting.

I'm glad we had decided to invite everyone back to our
house for lunch afterwards as it seemed like a gentle transition into the way forward – for life without Keziah. Despite
it being only just under two weeks since her birth, Mark was
due back to work the next day. Our intense time of grieving
together as a family unit was coming to an end, even though
it didn't seem long enough. When everyone left that afternoon, Josh fell asleep for a couple of hours, giving us a quiet
house to process our thoughts. Thinking over the events of
the day, Mark and I were both pretty subdued. That evening
we had a surprise visit from Carol, who had been one of my
best friends ever since we had worked together in the mission years previously, and her husband Andy. It was Carol's
birthday and they came bearing gifts in the form of Krispy
Kreme doughnuts. After the emotion of the day, it was just
what we needed to give us a little boost: food and friends!

Chapter 16

LIFE WITHOUT KEZIAH

Find rest, O my soul, in God alone;
my hope comes from him.
He alone is my rock and my salvation;
he is my fortress, I shall not be shaken.
My salvation and my honor depend on God;
he is my mighty rock, my refuge.
Trust in him at all times, O people;
pour out your hearts to him,
for God is our refuge.

(Psalm 62:5-8)

The following Monday, 13 October, almost a week after the funeral, was my thirty-seventh birthday. I was woken at 4.40 am by Josh – he had no idea it was my birthday! It was ironic. Usually I get so excited about my birthday that I'm awake at the crack of dawn. The one year I'm not so fussed, I get woken up while even the early morning chorus are still snoring!

My first (of many) birthday treats that day was the absence of a headache. Ever since Keziah had been born, almost three weeks ago now, I'd been taking painkillers every four hours during the day to numb the constant headache that had plagued me relentlessly. It increased during intense bouts of tears or as a result of lack of sleep. It was a physical sign of my grief. Mark and I both felt as if we were literally hanging on by the skin of our teeth. We missed little Kiki so much and at times the pain and loss were unbearable – our hearts felt as if they had been ripped apart. I was so conscious that the only way to get through this time victoriously was to just keep on running to God, for in His presence I found fullness of joy. It was bitter-sweet. My determination to work through the grief and not go under drove me to seek God with a desperation I had not experienced before. At the same time as feeling incredibly fragile and vulnerable, I had such a powerful sense of God Himself as my Rock. It was a real juxtaposition. I knew with a certainty that defied logic that I was held by God and that only in Him was my hope. I knew I had to just keep doing my part and continue making the decision to present myself before Him to encourage myself in Him and cover Mark with my prayers, to help him cope with the stress of work in addition to his grief.

I absolutely love the prayers of the apostle Paul, and two of the prayers in the book of Ephesians chapters one and three are particular personal favorites. A little phrase he uses in Ephesians 3:19 described what I was experiencing: "and to know this love that surpasses knowledge – that you may be filled to the measure of all the fullness of God." To explain this "knowledge," the Amplified Bible adds the words "through experience for yourselves." I was so enjoying experiencing God that it was taking the edge off my grief. I completely identified with a statement I read in a Phil Pringle book called *Inspired to Pray*:

> The times of suffering in a person's life can be the sweetest times in their life if they will draw near to God. Our connection with God deepens in suffering more than at any other time. How many times have I heard people

say that even though the time of trouble was terrible, it was also the richest time of their life?"

(Regal Books, 2009, p. 95)

This was true.

I had a real treat a week later when Pastor Bill, who was over in the UK, phoned to see how we were. Alan had told Pastor Bill what had happened. I was so blown away that he would take the time to phone that I was completely hyperactive for the rest of the day! He is such an inspiration. He just never gives up. Whatever obstacles are thrown across his path, he just keeps on going, moving mountains by his faith and winning people one by one into the Kingdom of God. I had just copied a couple of quotes from his book *Christianity in the Crosshairs* (Destiny Image, 2004) into my journal: "All the strength and force of man comes from his faith in things unseen. He who believes is strong; he who doubts is weak" (James Freeman Clarke) and "Faith is deliberate confidence in the character of God, whose ways you may not understand at the time" (Oswald Chambers).

I was still officially on maternity leave and was grateful for the time and space to grieve and allow God to restore my body and emotions. Whilst reading my Bible one day, I was struck by an interesting verse from Zechariah 9:12: "Return to the stronghold [of security and prosperity], you prisoners of hope" (AMP). I liked the idea of being a "prisoner of hope," held captive and unable to escape from the hope we were clinging to that, one day in the future, we would have another child. I knew we could not bring Keziah back, but we could hope and believe for another child, and in the meantime trust God and continue the adventure of faith by discovering new depths of His character. The moment my thoughts started to drag my emotions downward, I would instantly discipline myself to stop and return to my standpoint of Hope.

There were times over the next few months when I actually wondered if I was grieving properly. Is there such a thing as a "proper" way to grieve? I sensed such a grace from God over us which I knew was a really special gift. I was so thankful. Strangely though, I did expect the world to stop for a while and take time out with me, but of course it didn't. Life carried on. Josh had already changed since Keziah's birth. He was taller, chatting more and keeping us constantly amused with his daily antics. I felt much more protective over him and had to consciously hand over to God an irrational fear that kept trying to sneak in, that something would happen to him and we would lose him too.

We began planning the thanksgiving service that was due to be held on the first Saturday of December at our church. As the funeral was so small, we had decided to hold a public celebration of Keziah's life in my womb for the many friends and extended family that had stood with us, loved and supported us in so many ways. The service was to follow a similar format to the funeral with a few extra items. One of these was a DVD that Mark put together, compiled of short snippets from our video diary that we started shortly after receiving Keziah's diagnosis of Trisomy 18. (Mark had been really touched and inspired by a short film he had seen on the Trisomy 18 Foundation website about a little boy called Elliot. Elliot lived for ninety-nine days and his parents produced an incredibly moving tribute to his life on film.) We knew we would have some sort of service following Keziah's birth, whether it was to be a dedication of her life to God, as we had had for Josh, or a thanksgiving of the time she had been entrusted to us to look after. To have something tangible to work towards after the finality of the funeral was very therapeutic and helped us process our grief.

Before we knew it, it was the night before the service. Mark was coming home late, so, after putting Josh to bed,

I sat and listened to a talk on a CD given to us by a couple from church. The subject was how you react in your pivotal moments. The talk was based on John chapter 11, which is the account of the sisters Mary and Martha's conversations with Jesus before He raised their brother Lazarus from the dead. I noted down several of the key verses:

[Jesus] said, This sickness is not to end in death; but [on the contrary] it is to honor God and to promote His glory, that the Son of God may be glorified through (by) it. Now Jesus loved Martha and her sister and Lazarus. [They were His dear friends, and He held them in loving esteem.]

(John 11:4-5 AMP)

As I listened and wrote, I had a precious, unexpected encounter with God, in which I suddenly had such a sense of His sheer delight and pleasure over us. I felt He had allowed Keziah's life to be as it was, so that our faith, which is so precious to Him, might be revealed. I sensed the privilege of what we had been entrusted with.

[You should] be exceedingly glad on this account, though now for a little while you may be distressed by trials and suffer temptations, so that [the genuineness] of your faith may be tested, [your faith] which is infinitely more precious than the perishable gold which is tested and purified by fire. [This proving of your faith is intended] to redound to [your] praise and glory and honor when Jesus Christ (the Messiah, the anointed One) is revealed.

(1 Peter 1:6-7 AMP)

From the first moment on 1 May when we had been told that something was wrong with our unborn child, we had

wanted to honor God with our reaction to this news and
how we carried ourselves. Now, in the stillness of the room,
He spoke straight to my heart. I was silenced by His love and
overwhelmed by His incredible grace. Grace undeserved yet
abundantly poured out.

> You shall also be [so beautiful and prosperous as to be
> thought of as] a crown of glory and honor in the hand
> of the Lord, and a royal diadem [exceedingly beautiful]
> in the hand of your God.
>
> (Isaiah 62:3 AMP)

Jesus, Jesus, beautiful Savior. From the natural perspective
and in the eyes of this world, we had been through a sense-
less tragedy. My womb, full and fruitful for nine months, had
led to empty arms and an unused cot. Faith gives a different
perspective. In my mind, we had been given a precious piece
of God's heart. Through tragedy and suffering we had found
hidden in the darkness sparkling jewels of hope, priceless
treasures of faith and eternal measures of love.

Keziah's thanksgiving service the next day was such a
beautiful, special day. Bizarrely, in some ways, it felt as special as our wedding day as so many of our friends and family
had traveled to be there with us. My lingering memory of
the day was looking up into the sky and watching the forty-
one pink and white balloons we released, one for each week
Keziah was alive in my womb, disappear, up and up, higher
and higher...into heaven.

In John 11:40 Jesus promises Martha, "Did I not tell you
and promise you that if you would believe and rely on me,
you would see the glory of God?" (AMP). I believe we have
seen the glory of God through Keziah's life. May that grow
and continue throughout eternity.

Chapter 17

IONA MIA FAITH GRAYSON

———————————— ∿ ————————————

I was pushed back and about to fall,
but the Lord helped me.
The Lord is my strength and my song;
he has become my salvation.
Shouts of joy and victory resound in the tents of the righteous:
"The Lord's right hand has done mighty things!"
The Lord's right hand is lifted high;
the Lord's right hand has done mighty things!

(Psalm 118:15-16)

The first week of January 2009 brought with it the thrilling news that I was pregnant again. We were so excited that it had happened less than four months after Keziah's birth. All was well at the eight-week dating scan, so we were devastated to be told at the twelve-week scan that there was no heartbeat present. I was stunned to have lost yet another baby. We were advised to wait a while before trying once more for another child. I was reluctant at first, but seeing wisdom in this advice, we decided to put plans for another addition to our family on hold and enjoy the summer ahead. It meant I was free to help teach and leap about like crazy at our "Rock" children's camp, without fear of damaging an unborn life within.

Summer came and went, leaving in its wake the first anniversary of Keziah's birth/death day. With a heart full of poignant memories, I treated myself to a beautiful bunch of pink and white gerberas. Accompanied by Mum, Helen Mary and Josh, I traveled down to where we had scattered Keziah's ashes to reflect on the impact of her short time with us. When Mark returned from work, the three of us drove over to Beckenham crematorium, arriving at sunset to visit the little chapel of remembrance.

One week later, with the arrival of shorter days and autumnal weather, came the thrilling news that I was once again pregnant! From six weeks, I was given wonderful care and scanned every fortnight until we had passed the danger zone of the first trimester. Christmas and New Year celebrations followed shortly and time seemed to pass really quickly until we found ourselves back at the PRU Hospital on Thursday 21 January 2010, for the twenty-week antenatal ultrasound. We were ready and waiting to find out if our unborn child was a boy or girl. I desperately wanted a little girl but had convinced myself that a little brother for Josh would be equally as wonderful. We waited with bated breath as the sonographer investigated the life within. When she turned to us and smiled, saying, "You have a little girl!", my eyes immediately filled up with tears. I was so overwhelmed I couldn't speak. I just squeezed Mark's hand as we grinned insanely at each other! We were so thrilled! With the announcement of this news, we felt a milestone had been reached; healing and restoration had gone to the next level. Only another twenty weeks or so and we would meet this new daughter, a precious gift from God.

Armed with our exciting news, we rushed upstairs to the maternity ward where my old school friend from age five at Crofton Infant School, Lisa Lou, and her partner Stu had earlier that morning welcomed their twins into the world! As we gazed at Charlotte and Jack wrapped snugly in their cot, it seemed too good to be true that in the not-too-distant future we would be in their shoes, gazing at our own little pink bundle. (Just one for us though!) I could hardly contain myself!

It didn't take us long to buy our little girl her first set of pink babygros. Next step was to decide on her names. As I had chosen "Keziah," it was Mark's turn and he had already made up his mind! He had decided on the name "Iona." To begin with, I wasn't sure if I agreed, but I soon changed my mind when I discovered its meaning. In Greek Iona means "purple/violet-colored jewel." She would indeed be our precious little treasure. The color purple represents royalty in the Bible and we would bring Iona up to know her purpose, destiny and sense of worth as a daughter of the "King of Kings." Zechariah 9:16 tells us that God's people will "sparkle in his land like jewels in a crown" (NLT), and I began to speak this truth over Iona's life. Iona is also the name of an island in the Inner Hebrides that has a rich Christian heritage. We both agreed on Mia as a middle name, followed by Faith. Mia is the Scandinavian form of Mary and Mary in Hebrew means "wished for" or "desired" child. Very fitting. We followed this by Faith, for two reasons: it had taken faith to face yet another pregnancy, plus we wanted faith in God to be a foundational characteristic of her life. Iona Mia Faith Grayson: her names were chosen, we just had to wait for her arrival.

Now that we knew her name and gender, we started to prepare Josh for the arrival of his new little sister. By the time her due date came round in mid June, he was ready and waiting to fulfill his proud role of "Best Big Brother in the World!" Following the pattern of her siblings, Iona's due date came and went. I marked the day by holding two other long-awaited miracle newborn babies in my arms instead! Oliver George and Amelia Grace Thomson, our friends Carol and Andy's little arrivals, another set of twins, born the day before on Saturday 12 June. Iona already had a few new friends waiting to play but she was oblivious, too cosy inside to make her departure!

At forty-one weeks, I was given a date for induction – Thursday 24 June – if nothing happened naturally before that. The days passed with no indication that Iona was on her way, so with confirmation that there was a bed ready and waiting at the hospital, we dropped Josh off at Granny and Pa Pa's house, said goodbye and set off for the maternity ward with avid expectancy. I was hopeful things would get moving pretty quickly, but thirty-six hours later, now Friday evening, I was really disappointed to be told on examination that the gel induction had not made any difference. Although it was really lovely to see Sarah Hartson again, plus Ophelia (the Ghanaian midwife who looked after us the night we arrived at the start of Keziah's labor), I was beginning to dread each internal examination, plus I was desperately missing Josh. Already two days had passed in hospital and still no sign of Iona.

I don't know if my hormone levels were playing havoc with my emotions, but when Mark left me at 5 pm to go and collect Josh, I suddenly became really fearful. Every time I thought about the second part of labor, I felt a sense of dread. I'd struggled with that part during Josh's birth and it was also the point in labor with Keziah where, being in a "back to back" position, she had got stuck, her tiny heart had given up under the strain and she had died. Throughout this pregnancy with Iona, I had prayed specifically that God would help and guide me with the second stage of labor. For some reason, I had in my head that I wanted to do it in three pushes! I guess I thought two would be a bit quick and I didn't want to prolong it with four! Anyway, knowing that the birth would certainly come in the next day or so, I began to shake and cry. I didn't want to disturb the others in the ward, so I kept as quiet as possible. I texted a few people asking them to pray and kept repeating the words of Joshua 1:9 over and over to myself,

"Have I not commanded you? Be strong and courageous. Do not be terrified; do not be discouraged, for the Lord your God will be with you wherever you go."

I needed to counteract my fear with strength and courage. I didn't have it in me, but I believed God had an endless supply available that I could resource.

I needed to sleep and prepare myself for the labor sometime over the weekend, so I lay down and found a beautiful song from the Hillsong album *Faith+Hope+Love*, "I will exalt You," and played it on repeat with earphones.

I will exalt You
I will exalt You
I will exalt You
You are my God

My hiding place
My safe refuge
My treasure, Lord, You are
My friend and King
Anointed One
Most holy

Because You're with me
Because You're with me
Because You're with me
I will not fear

When the doctor came round at 10 pm, he advised that I be given another set of gel. However, when the midwife put me on a monitor, she decided against it, saying that there was already quite a lot of activity in my uterus and she didn't want to overstimulate it. She guessed that things would start naturally. I was relieved by her comments, stuck my earphones back in, and dozed in and out of sleep all night long, letting the words from "I will exalt You" sink into my subconscious. The line "Because You're with me, I will not fear" brought me peace as the Holy Spirit ministered to me through the song. I was safe in God's presence. I had chased the fear away. God would help me, I could relax.

At 3.43 am I woke up with a strong contraction. It was getting light outside, so I got up, made myself a cup of Earl Grey tea and waited to see how regular the contractions were. This was it. By 7 am I had moved to the labor ward, my waters had been broken by one of the doctors and Mark was on his way in!

During the week I had been in touch with Caroline, the midwife who had delivered Keziah and had been present as a student at Josh's birth. We really hoped she would be around for Iona's birth too. She was actually on annual leave but she said she really wanted to come into the hospital and be with us. The midwife in charge of us, Claire, had contacted Caroline and was keeping her informed of my progress. (Claire is Godmother to Caroline's daughter, so there was already a special connection there.)

By 11 am, I was still only 4 cm dilated, so the doctor advised a drip to speed up contractions. I was disappointed as I had my heart set on a water birth but I knew it was best to go with their advice. Once the drip was in, armed with gas and air, I was determined to remain upright.

I alternated between rocking backwards and forwards on the birthing ball and standing up and perching on the edge of a chair. Mark was highly amused as I kept repeating to myself a promise from Psalm 92:10 that I had learnt especially for labor:

...you have made me as strong as a wild ox,
You have anointed me with the finest oil. (NLT)

(After almost six years of marriage, he'd realized I was far from normal!)

Around 1 pm, Caroline arrived to join us. It was so lovely to see her and we were extremely touched that she had come in during her annual leave. She truly had gone over and above the call of duty. She said she could stay until about 2.40 pm and then would have to leave as she was off to view a house at 3 pm. The contractions were getting pretty intense by then and I was thankful for all my years of breathing exercises as a flautist. I knew the hours of long notes and tone exercises would come in handy at some point! I was breathing through the pain, counting the seconds, having mini competitions with myself and wondering how much more I would have to endure.

At 2.30 pm my legs were getting tired, so I asked for help to get onto the bed. I was aware that Caroline needed to leave in the next ten minutes. Still determined to stay upright, I bent over the back of the bed, facing away from Caroline, Claire and Mark. Instantly something changed. Suddenly the pain was continuous, with no break in between contractions. It was excruciating. The pain felt like a swirling vortex surrounding me and I was right in the center. I was in transition.

I knew the part I dreaded, the pushing stage, was next. This was the part I had prayed for specific help for. I could never have dreamed what would happen next. Looking back, I can truly say it was an Ephesians 3:20 experience:

Now to Him Who, by (in consequence of) the [action of His] power that is at work within us, is able to [carry out His purpose and] do superabundantly, far over and above all that we [dare] ask or think [infinitely beyond our highest prayers, desires, thoughts, hopes, or dreams]... (AMP)

I shouted out, "She's coming, I need to push." Right then, from deep within but as loud and clear as an audible voice,

I heard a man speaking, telling me what to do. "Wait, breathe, push," three specific commands. I knew instinctively it was the voice of the Holy Spirit. Ephesians 3:16 confirms His position within believers:

> May He grant you out of the rich treasury of His glory to be strengthened and reinforced with mighty power in the inner man by the [Holy] Spirit [Himself indwelling your innermost being and personality]. (AMP)

It wasn't Mark speaking and there was no other male present in the room.

I shouted out, "God is helping me!", then realized they wouldn't understand what I was saying. I was too preoccupied to go into the detail of what I was experiencing, so I just kept quiet and concentrated on the task at hand! (I checked with Mark afterwards and he said when I shouted out, the three of them just grinned at each other. I'm sure they thought I was hallucinating, but nothing had been more real in my life!)

Three times the voice spoke, guiding me. Three huge pushes later, at 2.41 pm on Saturday 26 June 2010, Iona Mia Faith Grayson was born, just in time for Caroline to deliver her and then leave to view a house! I was euphoric! I couldn't believe she was here, all whopping 9lb 2oz of her! What a gift – our little jewel Iona had arrived! After the fear I had experienced the previous night, followed by such an amazing, intimate experience hearing the Holy Spirit speak so clearly and the ease with which Iona finally arrived, I was truly overwhelmed.

> "My people will no longer be ashamed
> or turn pale with fear.
> For when they see their many children
> and all the blessings I have given them,
> they will recognize the holiness of the Holy One of Israel.
> They will stand in awe of the God of Jacob."
>
> (Isaiah 29:22-23 NLT)

My fear had given way to enormous blessing. To actually hold our little, soft, warm bundle alive in our arms and cuddle our newborn daughter gave us both such immense joy and a sense of tremendous awe at how God had restored us and made our family complete: Mark, myself, Josh and Iona here together on earth and little Keziah up in heaven, perfect and healed, with whom we would one day be reunited.

In 1 Corinthians 13:13 it says:

And now these three remain: faith, hope and love. But the greatest of these is love.

God's love had never failed us. It sustained us through the tough times and carried us through to victory. Along the way, we had learnt some powerful lessons. Never give up on your dreams. Don't give in to negative emotions but strengthen your Spirit until you soar. Trust in the Word of God and remember: "Everything is possible for him who believes" (Mark 9:23). Always give God room to have the last word. He will never fail you and He is well able.

True to His character, God had proved Himself faithful in our lives. I want to thank you for taking time to read our story. I pray that it has inspired you, encouraged you and given you hope.

SALVATION

If you have read my book and would like to know more about having a relationship with God through Jesus Christ, I would encourage you to buy a Bible and, starting at the book of John in the New Testament, begin to read it, asking God to reveal Himself to you.

The Bible clearly teaches that Jesus is the way, the truth and the life and no one comes to God except through Him (John 14:6). Only Jesus has the power to give each one of us a fresh start here on earth with God, which is the beginning of a wonderful relationship that will continue throughout eternity.

If you have never accepted Jesus Christ for yourself as your own personal Lord and Savior, I would encourage you to make that decision now by speaking out loud the following prayer and believing it in your heart:

Father God, I come to You now in the name of Jesus. I want to begin a new life journey with You today. I acknowledge that You are the one true God and that I have sinned against You by choosing to live life my own way without You. Today I make a choice to turn away from that lifestyle. I ask for Your forgiveness. I acknowledge that Jesus Christ died on the cross to take the punishment for my sins. Please forgive me and wipe away my past mistakes by the power of Your blood shed on the cross for me. Today I make You my Lord and Savior, and I want to spend the rest of my life on an exciting journey of discovering who You are and Your purpose for my life. Thank You, Father God, for what You have done for me. In Jesus' name, Amen.

If you have prayed that prayer, it is essential that you find a good Bible-believing church where you can meet with other believers who can encourage you and help you in your new God Adventure.

I would love to hear from you too. Please contact me at the following address: lizzie@keziahbook.co.uk

FOR THOSE WHO MAY HAVE
TERMINATED A PREGNANCY

I believe that from the moment of conception, life begins: unseen, hidden and minute, yet intricately designed and formed by Almighty God. Psalm 139 testifies to the creative miracle of human life:

> For you created my inmost being;
> you knit me together in my mother's womb.
> I praise you because I am fearfully and wonderfully made;
> your works are wonderful, I know that full well.
> My frame was not hidden from you
> when I was made in the secret place.
> When I was woven together in the depths of the earth,
> your eyes saw my unformed body.
> All the days ordained for me were written in your book
> before one of them came to be.

(vv. 13-16)

When faced with the option to terminate my pregnancy with Keziah, as medically we were repeatedly told her condition deemed her "incompatible with life," I strongly felt that this was not my decision to make. The Holy Spirit instantly reminded me of Deuteronomy 30:19-20:

> This day I call heaven and earth as witnesses against you that I have set before you life and death, blessings and curses. Now choose life, so that you and your children may live and that you may love the Lord your God, listen to his voice, and hold fast to him.

When given the choice between life and death for my unborn child, I was urged to "choose life" and then step out in faith, trusting in God for the consequences of my choice. I know without a shadow of doubt that God gave me the grace and strength to walk through each day that followed. I could not have done it in my own strength. At that stage of my life, I was able to hear His voice, recognize what He wanted me to do and carry out His command. It was all by His grace, walking step by step in the knowledge of His love for me. My rock and foundation was the knowledge and experience of God's love, without which I would not have survived.

You may have been faced with a similar decision and taken the alternative route with your pregnancy and chosen to terminate. It may have been a recent experience or one taken years previously. You may have questioned your decision and battled with the endless "what ifs?" or you may have found peace and not given it another thought.

I wanted to write a message of hope for those in the former group, who may be plagued with doubts, guilt, shame and regret. Whatever is in our past, God's love, forgiveness and healing are far greater than anything we can ever imagine. The finished work of Jesus' death on the cross covers every choice we make that goes against God's commands. It must, however, be applied to our life, and for that to happen we have to invite Him to come and bring His forgiveness, cleansing and healing.

The Holy Spirit is ready and willing right now to take away the effects of any decision you may have made that has grieved God and caused you to suffer. He can replace the pain with a freedom and love that may be inconceivable to you right now. In John 14:26-7 Jesus explained:

> "the Counselor, the Holy Spirit, whom the Father will send in my name, will teach you all things and will remind you of everything I have said to you. Peace I leave with you; my peace I give you. I do not give to you as the world gives. Do not let your hearts be troubled and do not be afraid."

God loves you. Three simple, life-changing words. If you will open your heart and allow the Holy Spirit to make them more than just words on a page and the beginning of a transforming love affair between yourself and the Creator of the Universe, your Heavenly Father, then the first step of healing has begun. Jesus throws out His invitation to you in Matthew 11:28:

> "Come to me, all you who are weary and burdened and I will give you rest."

He doesn't condemn you; He offers mercy, understanding and compassion. God's forgiveness is immediate. In 1 John 1:9 it says:

> If we confess our sins, he is faithful and just and will forgive us our sins and purify us from all unrighteousness.

Although we may believe that God's forgiveness is available, the hardest thing is often to forgive ourselves. We tend to re-play the past over and over in our minds and build up layer upon layer of guilt and shame. A friend once painted a helpful mental image, of which I often remind myself when caught in the trap of constantly replaying the past. Once

I had asked God's forgiveness, he told me to picture myself throwing the situation into a big lake and planting a "No Fishing" sign next to the water. Under no conditions was I allowed to get my fishing rod out and pull out what I had thrown in!

It may be important for you to ask the baby you terminated for forgiveness. Their chance to live was taken away through no fault of their own. Picture that little one safe and well, wrapped and snuggled in the arms of Jesus, or perhaps as the two-, three-, four-year-old or whatever age they would be now. Jesus said,

> "Let the little children come to me, and do not hinder them, for the kingdom of heaven belongs to such as these."
>
> (Matthew 19:14)

As you ask forgiveness, wait quietly and the Holy Spirit may give you a picture or vision of your little one, safe and at peace.

During weeks 6–7 after conception, the baby is about the size of a kidney bean. The tiny heart is beating and the head is taking shape. Other crucial organs are forming such as the kidneys and liver. By 11–12 weeks, the baby's organs have formed. He\she is able to suck, chew and swallow. Even toenails and fingernails are beginning to form. The baby is a miniature of what he/she would be at birth six months later, except for being a tiny size. The baby is also a spiritual being. His\her spirit is eternal and lives on in the Kingdom of Heaven, safe in the presence of God. Whatever choices you may have made concerning the unborn child, know with complete certainty that your child is not suffering any more. Nor do you need to. I love the New Living Translation version of Revelation 21:3-4:

I heard a loud shout from the throne, saying, "Look, God's home is now among his people! He will live with them, and they will be his people. God himself will be with them. He will wipe away every tear from their eyes, and there will be no more death or sorrow or crying or pain. All these things are gone forever."

God Himself will wipe every tear away. In Him there is hope, forgiveness, healing, joy and eternal life. Your unborn treasure is safe in heaven. There is no need to suffer any more. Jesus came to give you a "rich and satisfying life" (John 10:10 NLT). His abundant life means that you can have hope instead of hopelessness, peace instead of pain and joy instead of sadness. It can begin today.

METRO MINISTRIES

Metro Ministries is a Christian, non-profit organization dedicated to serving inner-city children throughout the five boroughs of New York City and in various urban centers around the world. The organization was established in 1980 and has been serving low-income, inner-city children and their families for more than a quarter of a century.

17 Menahan Street
Brooklyn, NY 11221
Phone: 718-453-3352
email:info@metroministries.org

For more information about Metro Ministries, Pastor Bill Wilson or sponsoring a child, please see www.metroministries.org

Lynda

From accident & trauma to healing & wholeness

By Lynda Scott

List Price: £9.99 / $15.99 / 176 pages

This book is a moving story of courage and faith in overcoming personal tragedy. It has the capacity to transform your understanding of healing and give hope to those in need. Following a life-changing accident, Lynda retells the dramatic story that led to the powerful ministry that amazed witnessing doctors. Her miraculous physical and emotional healing restored her to life and gave her back the hope of marriage and family.

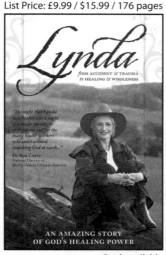

eBook available

Lynda's story demonstrates how God brought supernatural healing to every part of her spirit, soul and body. Profound spiritual principles become clear as she tells what God did in her life. This book is not only a wonderful celebration of her healing, it's also an enormous encouragement to all who would step forward in faith and put their trust in God.

"My faith was strong before, but it rose to a whole new level after seeing Lynda's healing."
Dr Gregory Foote M.B., B.S., F.R.A.C.G.P.

"The Lord ministered to her [Lynda], systematically healing one part of her body after another. As a physiotherapist, I was amazed."
Roslyn Curry – Physiotherapist

"Learning that trauma is experienced at all levels of our body, soul and spirit was a transformational concept for me... The atmosphere in the room at the time of healing was one of awe."
Dr Catherine Hayes B. Med. [Hons.], Newcs., D.R.C.O.G.[U.K.], Dip. Psych.Onc.[Melb.]

Frida

Chosen to die, Destined to Live

By Frida Gasumba

List Price: £8.99 / $14.99 / 176 pages

eBook available

Frida witnessed her family being massacred by Hutu men with machetes and was then asked how she wanted to die. She could not afford a bullet, which they offered to sell her, so instead received what should have been a fatal blow to the head. She was put in a mass grave with her slaughtered family only to find herself still alive and conscious. She eventually climbed out of the pit covered in filth and blood. Frida's traumas would never be undone, but today this young woman has an important message for the world. This book tells the true, dramatic story of life amid the horror of genocide, but more importantly how Frida's life was utterly transformed by the power to forgive and love her enemies. Amazingly, in the midst of the traumas she found Christ. Her story is for all those who have gone through life shattering experiences and are unable to forgive, imprisoned by bitterness and distress. The message is one of immense hope and personal deliverance pointing towards the transforming power of forgiveness. She was chosen to die, yet destined to live the fruit of her transformation is expressed in Frida's present day work with the orphans of Rwanda.

"This book demonstrates the depths of human depravity and witnesses to the triumph of grace, love and forgiveness through Christ. An inspiration."
**The Most Reverend and Right Honourable
John Mugabi Tucker Sentamu**

THE STORY OF A MIRACULOUS ESCAPE FROM THE RWANDAN GENOCIDE

Sarah

From an abusive childhood and the depths of suicidal despair to a life of hope and freedom

By Sarah Shaw

List Price: £8.99 / $14.99 / 176 pages

From an abusive childhood and the depths of suicidal despair to a life of hope and freedom
Sarah Shaw looked in control of her life. She had a successful career as a manager in retail business. But she came to a point when she could no longer keep up appearances, by controlling her tormented inner world. So explosive was her inner pain, and so damaged was she by the consequences of childhood abuse, that she was eventually put on a lifetime's incapacity benefit. Her consultant psychiatrist was at a loss how to help. This story is not, however, about the horrors of abuse, but is an extraordinary testimony to the triumph of God's healing love.

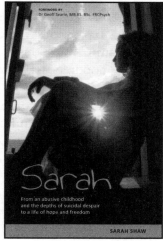

eBook available

The author writes:
"So many abused, hurting people don't understand their brokenness. They are stuck, as I was, in the tormenting symptoms of guilt, self-hatred, multiple fears, depression, Obsessive Compulsive Disorder, eating disorders, self-harming and suicidal tendencies. The book gives insights into the Christian healing ministry I received and offers hope to victims of abuse, without negating the reality of the desperate inner conflicts and struggles."

"This remarkable book is about true recovery of health by a deeply wronged woman, whom I met more than ten years ago. Rarely is this subject written about, and even more uncommonly in Sarah's calm and thoughtful way."
Dr Geoff Searle MBBS. BSc. FRCPsych (Sarah's Pychiatrist)

"So many people around the world have been abused, and often their pain is muffled by secrecy. Thankfully the woman who wrote this book has decided to expose her pain to the light of Jesus Christ. By doing so she has found total healing – and I believe her decision to share her painful secret with the world will help many other abused people find complete emotional recovery."
J. Lee Grady – Editor, Charisma Magazine

We hope you enjoyed reading this
Sovereign World book.
For more details of other Sovereign
books and new releases see our website:

www.sovereignworld.com

You can also join us on Facebook and Twitter.
To promote this title kindly consider writing
a comment on our website or Facebook page, or at
goodreads.com, shelfari.com and Amazon.

Our authors welcome your feedback on their books.
Please send your comments to our offices at:

Sovereign World Ltd, PO Box 784,
Ellel, Lancaster, LA1 9DA, United Kingdom
info@sovereignworld.com

Sovereign World titles are available from
all good Christian bookshops.

For information about our international distributors visit:
www.sovereignworld.com / trade

If you would like to help us send a copy of this book and
many other titles to needy pastors in developing countries,
please write for further information or send your gift to:

Sovereign World Trust, PO Box 777,
Tonbridge, Kent TN11 0ZS
United Kingdom
www.sovereignworldtrust.org.uk

The Sovereign World Trust is a registered charity